Compensatory Education

MOSES J. NTUK-IDEM

SAXON HOUSE

© M.J. Ntuk-Idem 1978

British Library Cataloguing in Publication Data

Ntuk-Idem, Moses J

    Compensatory education.
    1. Compensatory education — England — London
    2. Socially handicapped children — Education —
    England — London
    3. Education, Urban — England — London
    I. Title   LC4096.G7

    ISBN 0-566-00226-4

Published by

SAXON HOUSE, Teakfield Limited,
Westmead, Farnborough, Hants., England

Reprinted 1979

ISBN 0 566 00226 4

Printed in Great Britain by
Ilfadrove Limited, Barry, Glamorgan, S.Wales

Contents

Acknowledgement   vii

Introduction   1

1 BACKGROUND   7

Some account of the controversy of educational
inequality   7

The measured differences between black and
white pupils on test scores   14

A review of compensatory education   16

Two cases and their implications   26

2 METHOD   30

Description of the study   30

The operational design   30

The training activity   35

3 RESULTS   38

The characteristics of the participants   38

Analysis of test scores   44

Test of treatment effect in 1972   47

Test of treatment effect in 1973   50

The 1972 social adjustment study   59

The 1972 sociometric study   63

Analysis of expenditure pattern of the projects   71

Contextual analysis   73

The evaluation of the training activity   77

4   DISCUSSION   80

The limitation of the research   80

The research and the Headstart programmes   84

Gain   88

5   SUMMARY   105

Appendices   108

Bibliography   143

Acknowledgement

This study could not have been carried out without help from many individuals and agencies. The research has been funded by the Urban Programme, Community Relations Commission now known as The Commission for Racial Equality, Community Service Volunteers and Local Authorities. Dr A. Little, Dr A. Sumner, Mr P. Spink, Mr W. Van der Eyken, Dr C. Bagley and Dr P. Quinn gave useful advice at various stages of the study and head teachers, parents, teachers, pupils and many others not mentioned gave valuable support. In acknowledging all this help, the author accepts full responsibility for the final product.

Introduction

The study falls into five chapters: the background, method, result, discussion and summary. In Chapter 1, some statements have been made about the study criterion and relevant studies have been reviewed. In Chapter 2, an attempt has been made to describe the study design and Chapter 3 is devoted to the results. Evidence relevant to practical application, and the contribution of the study to methodology and theory have also been specified. In Chapter 4 some attempts have been made to interpret and qualify the results, to indicate the implications and to suggest further research areas. The final chapter gives a summary of the main findings.

The research criterion relates to the phenomenon of the inequality of educational chances. The compensatory education programme has been applied as a 'model' for treating basic skills associated with levels of educational attainment. The research interest stems partly from recorded knowledge of the existence of a discrepancy in educational chances between certain categories of socio-economic status groups, and partly from a recognition of the failure of the formal education system in England, in the last half century, to correct such disparities.

Some accounts have been given in the review of the interest which has been stimulated by the problem of inequality and on the nature of the link between nature, nurture and intelligence. Sociological and psychological studies which have been carried out since World War II have suggested that educational experience has had a minimal effect on low socio-economic status groups. Evidence indicates that, on the whole, only a small proportion of working class children have been able to benefit from extended schooling and that even fewer have had access to higher education. The cause of this has been thought to be linked partly with

genetic factors and partly with the restricted aims of
education, with its bias in favour of a selected
minority drawn largely from the middle class.
Educationalists and researchers have attempted to
redress the imbalance by resorting to measures which
have placed importance on the effect of nurturing as a
criterion for raising the cognitive threshold level of
the disadvantaged pupils. This strategy has given rise
to a number of experiments with enrichment programmes
and compensatory education is one form of such an
experiment. In the present study, it is hoped that
some contribution will be made to the understanding of
both the strategies for raising the level of basic
educational skills and of evaluating the nature of the
link between environmental factors and educational
attainment.

As stated previously, the introductory chapter sets
out the strategy for the study and establishes some
criteria for testing the effects of the compensatory
treatment. The Headstart programme and literature
review have been included in this chapter. Home and
school factors which have been reported to correlate
with educational attainment have also been examined.
The review of some of the studies on colour differences seems to support the superiority of whites over
blacks on measures of intelligence, in spite of
Pidgeon's contrary evidence and the limited value of
most of the intelligence test instruments in use. The
research is important in providing a model for a
creative and stimulating educational support by
teachers and other professional workers concerned with
play schemes, summer schools and social education in
schools.

Chapter 2 of the book has concentrated mainly on
methodology, structural design, treatment procedure,
measuring instruments and evaluation technique. The
present method of study was adopted in order to overcome some of the factors which limited the impact of
many of the Headstart programmes on cognitive gains.
It also took account of the crucial problem of
exploiting statistically the technique of randomisation

in social science experiments and the design benefited greatly from the work done by Campbell and Stanley. The technique adopted in designing the operational workshops in the study has proved a useful model for replication studies which can be applied at different levels of educational activity. The method of learning by discovery used throughout the programme constituted an important contrast to the pedagogic mode of teaching usually associated with formal education. The design model has made some significant implications for the motivation, organisation and arrangement of knowledge for team work. The importance of training has been treated severely in the text and the nature of the relationship between teachers' quality, planned operation on the one hand and pupils achievement on the other has also been covered.

The study has thrown up a number of interesting factors. Some factorial differences between black and white parents and their children have been recorded. The immigrant pupils have been found to differ from the English ones in their level of IQ scores, even though some similarities appeared with their parents on measures of SES. The strength of the gains achieved have been critically analysed in the text and the overall evidence of the study indicates that the West Indian pupils as a group were more deficient in basic educational skills than the non West Indian ones. The child and sociometric studies included provided additional data for analysis and the advantages gained by using these instruments have been stated in the book. Some excursions have been made into policy implications of the evidence. The analysis of income and expenditure has pointed to some relationship between teachers' quality and learning effectiveness. This evidence supports the importance that Coleman attached to teachers' quality in his report. The implications of this factor on resource allocation have been stated in the study. The contextual analysis included has highlighted the 'flood gate' phenomenon usually experienced with socially and educationally deprived children.

Chapter 4 on discussion, has helped to demonstrate some of the limitations of the study, and has indicated the need to be more vigorous with operational models directed towards the treatment of educational deficits. For instance, the problem raised by Cain and Watts that the raising of the mean level of learning might occur at the expense of widening the distribution has been recognised in the study. One main contribution of the study is the reflection of the point that compensatory programmes could provide a useful basis for stimulating pupils learning. But the question of the adequate age for effective intervention requires further studies. The usefulness of making provisions available for early schooling and family support has been suggested by Pringle et al. The experience of this study indicates that in order for some of the deprived families to be able to make an adequate use of treatment provisions the government might need to offer some form of disposable income to parents in Educational Priority Areas, with children below school age at a level necessary and sufficient to motivate commitment without destroying their incentives to self autonomy and choice.

The concept of action research is used here to mean a form of applied research which is clinical in its design but conducted under conditions similar to actual practice. The choice of this clinical technique of research design with respect to the experimentation on cognitive learning is directed towards overcoming some of the inherent limitations usually associated with experimentation in human sciences. Ausubel, (1969) pointed out that the study of phenomena in human sciences was punctuated with problems of design, control and measurement. The nature of some of these methodological design problems have been highlighted in the study. The concept of compensatory education relates to a form of educational treatment designed to improving cognitive achievement defects which are primarily environmentally induced. It differs from either special or remedial education. Special education usually refers to provision for meeting the needs of children with recognised handicaps and remedial

4

treatment is associated with measures adopted to helping children who have fallen behind in their school
work but who are considered capable of reaching a
higher standard with appropriate assistance. Different
shades of meaning have been given to compensatory
education. Historically the Headstart programmes
brought it into fashion and functionally, Sprehe et at.
(1969) argued that compensatory education could compensate putative deficiencies in learning, modify
behaviour and influence educational systems. Such an
instrumental notion of compensatory education has
become associated with treating specific types of
environmental factors associated with educational
attainment. Smiley (1967) interpreted this in terms of
the improvement of environmental deficits in the homes,
neighbourhood and school which have retarded and
limited educational progress. Hubbard (1971) pointed
out that the stimulation caused by compensatory treatment could break the cycle of disadvantage.

THE RESEARCH STATEMENT

The action aspect of the programme was aimed at raising
the level of cognitive attainment of the selected
pupils and the research function was directed towards
designing a method to monitor and measure the effect of
the treatment. The action research studies were undertaken in the summers of 1970, 1971, 1972, 1973, 1974
and 1976 in Lambeth, Islington, Hackney, Runnymede and
Surrey Heath respectively. The 1970 project was held
at the project centre and in 1971 in a primary school.
The 1972 project was held at a church and the 1973,
1974 and 1976 ones took place at a youth and community
centre.

In 1970 the author was appointed to a project in a
multi-racial borough of London. The project was set up
jointly by the borough and the Inner London Education
Authority with the help of Urban Programme grants. It
was set up to meet the socio-educational needs of
'unattached' adolescents. In order to understand some
of the needs a pilot study of the current provisions

5

for adolescents in the area was undertaken by the
author. The study indicated that provisions of some
facilities such as housing and recreation were
inadequate in meeting the needs of these young people.
This lack of facilities was made more noticeable by the
disproportionate concentration of immigrant population
in the area. The school aspect of the study indicated
that school resources in the area were inadequate in
meeting the problems associated with a high concentration of immigrant pupils. One head teacher reported
that most of the West Indian pupils, who formed the
majority of the school immigrant population,
experienced severe learning difficulties. The author
presented a report to the borough and with the support
of the Department of Education and Science, a decision
was taken to implement an educational programme that
could raise the pupil's level of performance. The 1970
project was funded by Community Service Volunteers and
this limited the pilot study to a week but it became
possible as a result of this study to obtain major
grants from the Urban Programme, the Inner London
Education Authority and the Community Relations
Commission for the 1971 and 1972 studies. In the 1973
and 1974 studies grants came from Surrey Education
Committee, Chertsey Urban District Council now known as
Runnymede District Council and parents. The 1976 study
was paid for wholly by parents. The need to design the
study systematically necessitated an appraisal of the
problems of educational inequality and a review of some
studies of compensatory education programmes. The
review in Chapter 1 indicates the nature of these
problems.

1 Background

1.1 SOME ACCOUNT OF THE CONTROVERSY OF EDUCATIONAL INEQUALITY

The changing interpretations of the concept of equality of educational opportunity and the increasing attempt to investigate systematically the consequences of educational activity have created a new interest in the nature of the relationship between environment, heredity and educational attainment. Some environmentalists with the nurturing view such as Helevtius and Watson have argued that all children are blessed with equal cognitive endowment. This implies that with an adequate nurturing technique all children should be able to benefit from schooling. Others such as Halsey, Butcher, Klineberg and Jencks have stressed the importance of environment in educational attainment. The geneticists in their rhetoric which started in about 1869 with Francis Galton's book have argued that innate ability is a major achievement factor. Burt reinforced this position, not without intense criticisms, by suggesting that about 90% of intelligence was inherited. Jensen interpreting both from his studies and from Burt's work argued that the heritability of intelligence was 80%. This meant that genetic differences accounted for differences in measured ability.

Fehr and Helsers amongst others criticised the basis of Jensen's evidence. Fehr's replication analysis of Jensen's work resulted in 38% variability of genetic components. Helsers (1969) criticised Jensen also on the ground that Jensen misrepresented his findings. The Milwaukee project connected with this contained a large proportion of retarded children which was bound to affect the rate of improvement. Vernon stated that the effect of genes was not indisputable, and that Jensen did not take sufficient account of the effect of mother - child interaction on intelligence. Previous estimate by Burt (1958) indicated that heredity accounted for 82% and environment 18% of the variance in intelligence. Jencks on the other hand, stipulated 40% heritability, 54% environment and 6% interaction. Skeels (1966) reported that environmental treatment could change intelligence quotient (IQ) by 20 to 30 points. Jenson (1968) replied to this by saying that the contrasting statements between Burt and Skeels could be reconciled by the hypothesis that environment acted as a threshold variable thus suggesting that further environmental stimulation would add negligible increments to mental ability. Besides the conflicting statements on the proportionate effects of genes and environment on measured ability, serious doubts have been expressed on the efficiency of ability scales.

Eysenck (1971) and Butcher (1968) maintained that intelligence scales measured only one aspect of mental ability. Englemann (1969) suggested that the trichotomy of ability included cognitive, affective and psychomotor aspects and that most intelligence scales have tended to discriminate in favour of the cognitive domain. The affective factor has proved more difficult to measure. The Scottish Council (1953) made the point that the criterion for judging the effect of either nature or nurture on ability was inadequate. Cavalli-Storza (1970) made a similar point. Butcher (1968) argued that any report of the proportions of genetic and environmental factors on intelligence should be treated with reservation. Besides the problem of the unidimensionality of intelligence scales, some evidence of social class differences on test scores have been reported. Terman and Merill (1937) reported that 30% of IQ was associated with socio-economic status (SES) Jencks put this at 0.35. Jensen argued that heredity which determined IQ differences was a function of social class. Jensen's model of the dependence of intelligence on heredity could be misleading in the sense that correlated factors did not necessarily establish casual relationships. Butcher (1968) and Cavalli-Storza (1970) pointed out the limitation of extrapolating results derived from the study of animals in predicting human

8

behaviour and the inherent weakness of making
inferences from the study of twins. Brierley (1973)
and Jensen reported that undernourishment could reduce
IQ score. This adds a further dimension to the
variables affecting cognitive gains.

Besides the conflicting accounts reported above,
Jencks made the point that heritability was in itself
an average applied only to groups and this constituted
a major weakness. Jencks said that the available
knowledge was fuzzy and that verbal and general ability
while tending to correlate highly with IQ scores, reading and mathematics have tended to show less relationship both to IQ and to SES. The above account
indicates that the evidence relating to the effect of
nature and nurture on performance might have been
influenced to a certain extent by value judgement.
Chronsley (1972) made similar observations. For
practical purposes, Butcher recommended that educational planning should take environment as the crucial
variable. This position has led to the renewed
interest in the study of the main environmental
variables such as school and home, which are associated
with cognitive achievement. The next section will
indicate the major school and home factors associated
with cognitive performance. The analysis of school
factors covers the effects of selection, organisation,
attitude, school mix, peer group, mental ability, early
improvement on attainment and date of enrolment.

School effects

Evetts (1970) reported that selectivity and differential treatment had exacerbated educational inequality
thus creating social injustice and economic waste. In
the UK some schools are streamed on the basis of 11+
selection and in the USA tracking is usually associated
with this form of school organisation based on ability.
Butcher (1968) argued that the grouping by ability did
disfavour low ability groups and that the organisation
of secondary education into three distinct kinds of
schools, providing different kinds of education seemed
basically indefensible. Agmer and Vernon said that the

selection by ability test was biased in favour of those
with cognitive skills and the intensive treatment, in
terms of nurturing cognitive skills, of those selected
would tend to result in a greater inequality.
Gurney-Dixon (1954) stated that educational selection
had increased the handicaps of the working class
pupils. Coleman (1966), Floud (1961), Yates (1966),
Turner (1961), Pace (1963), NFER studies, Gurney-Dixon
(1954), Crowther (1959 and 1960), Newson (1963),
Robbins (1963 and 1964) and Plowden (1967) pointed out
the problems associated with the widening of the gap
between the middle and working classes with respect to
access to higher education and to educational achievement. Jackson rejected some of the conclusions on the
effect of selection by stating that the effects of
streaming and curriculum placement had not been substantiated conclusively. Some other researchers have
indicated also that streaming did not appear to
increase inequality of test scores significantly and in
other cases a mixed ability grouping has been found to
result in mixed effects on both the deprived and the
non deprived students. The NFER data collected between
1964 and 1967 showed that students in fast streams were
two points ahead of those in slow streams and one point
difference between the two in curriculum orientation.
In contrast to the above, Floud, Halsey and Martin
argued that social class attitude rather than selection
had affected educational opportunity strongly.
Rosenthal and Jackson (1968), Burstall (1968), Flowers
(1968), Lunn (1970), Bagley (1968) reported that
teachers' attitude was of paramount importance in
school achievement. Townsend (1973) said that the conflicting attitudes of teachers to different groups of
pupils had tended to intensify inequality, for example,
teachers expected the West Indian pupils to fail and
they did so. Butcher described this tendency as the
phenomenon of the self fulfilling prophecy.

On the effect of school mix and peer group, Jencks
(1973), Sewell and Armer and Hauser (1966) stated that
the mixing of different social groups in schools did
not have effects on student aspiration. This has
tended to conflict with Coleman's evidence of the

sponsorship effect of the priviledged schools, although Banks and Finlayson's findings have supported the discovery of low achievement by the working class pupils who attended grammar schools, with high achievement of the similar group who went to comprehensive schools. Of the elements of school, Labov (1973), Gans (1962) and Wilmott (1966) reported that peer group influence could prove a powerful influence in schools. The effect of early mental functioning and the date of starting school have been associated also with educational chances.

Wilson stated that the initial mental ability of pupils at the primary school level accounted for more of the individual differences in subsequent school programme than any other single variable. Some research studies have indicated also that pupils who started school in Summer have tended to do less well than the Spring or Autumn starters. Bloom (1964) reported that the measured ability at four years of age has tended to predict attainment at the age of seven. Banks and Finlayson reported on the predictive property of initial ability. Kagan (1973), on the other hand, reported that performance of juniors on test scores could not predict permanent ability trait, since children differed with respect to Piaget's stages of cognitive development. Arnett (1969) stated also that early improvement would not always be maintained. Jencks argued that the apparent predictive role of initial ability was less the result of limitation on the part of the pupils and more the direct consequence of the zero effect of schooling on the cognitive development of some of the pupils. The conflicting evidence of school effect on learning appears to reflect the effect of methodological differences.

This conflicting evidence has made it more difficult to draw any firm conclusions on the relationship between teaching method, selection and school organisation on the one hand, and cognitive gains on the other. For example, Peaker reported that teaching was less effective than home in influencing performance. Coleman (1966), Jencks (1973), Little (1971) and

11

Burgess (1973) argued that school reform and compensatory treatment have tended to have a limited effect on
inequality. On the other hand, Banks and Finlayson
(1973), Rutter, Yule and Berger (1974) found some cases
in which schools affected attainment significantly and
in which differential treatment has tended to compensate the top streams at the expense of the bottom ones.
Banks and Finlayson's study indicated that the top
stream of the SES five has tended to do worse in the
grammar schools than their counterpart in the
comprehensive schools and that the 'sunken' middle
class accounted for the success in the comprehensive
schools. On the question of access to higher education
by the working class pupils, Westergaard and Little,
Jackson, Marsden, Moberg, Havighurst and Furneaux
studies showed the under-representation of this group
in higher education. Banks and Finlayson, Halsey and
Martin (1957), Fraser (1959), Wiseman (1964) and
Douglas (1964) linked this under-representation with
selection. The Robbins committee showed also that
class bias was an inherent part of the British system
of education. Jencks suggested that since school
reform did not yield the expected social change for the
deprived pupils, it would be justifiable therefore to
offer some positive support to this group. Some
account of studies of home effect on educational
chances is reviewed below in order to provide a pers-
pective of the major environmental variables associated
with cognitive gains.

Home effects

The major variables of the home factors associated with
school attainment include poor housing, education and
occupation of parents, family size, relationship and
structure, patterns of language and child development
and institutional support. Douglas (1964) reported
that poor housing had adverse effects on test scores.
Ault (1940), Fraser (1959), NFER and Crowther reported
that parents occupation influenced test scores.
Gurney-Dixon (1954), Plowder (1967), Dale and Griffith,
Hyman, Sewell and Shah (1968), Douglas, Floud, Swift,
Brierley, Banks (1973) and Fraser (1967) all reported

12

that parents education, attitude to, beliefs and values
of and interest in school and the encouragement that
these parents gave to their children affected test
scores. Metcalfe (1950), Winterbottom, Newson (1963)
and Drew and Tsaham (1957) reported that emotional link
between parents and their children affected school
performance. Klein, Crutchley and Tapper (1967),
Swift, Peaker (1971), Banks (1971) and Plowden reported
that socialisation pattern was a factor in educational
achievement. Bernstein, Swanson (1960), Newson and
Newson (1968), Brandis and Henderson (1970), Boehm and
Nass (1962), Kohn (1959) and Jackson and Marsden (1962)
reported that the positive support given by the middle
class parents to their children on reasoning, exploration, verbalisation and emotion together with emphasis
on toys affected performance.

Douglas (1964), Crowther, Stott (1956), Dale and
Greenald (1955), Nisbet (1953), Floud, Plowden, Rutter
(1973) and Wedge and Prosser (1973) reported that
family size has tended to correlate with school performance negatively. McCarthy (1946), Day (1932), Davis
(1937) and Peaker (1971) reported that besides the
family size factor, adult - child interaction affected
language development. Davis (1973) found some association between smoking in pregnancy and sensory
development.

On the institutional factors, Jackson (1973) reported
that some methods of institutional care could and did
increase deprivation especially of the West Indian
pupils. This tended to formalise as a situation in
which the social system expected a child of a mental
parent to have nervous complications, expected a black
child to be less able and used the educational system
to confirm these attitudes.

Gurney-Dixon (1966) stated that adverse home factors
had resulted in the deterioration of working class
pupils after a good start at eleven and in the subsequent improvement of middle class ones after a poor
start at the same age. Swift reported that part of the
variability in performance between the classes was

associated with discontinuity between the working class homes and the school. Douglas, and Ross and Simpson (1968) indicated that these depressive factors had resulted in a permanent disparity in educational attainment between the middle and the working classes. In this process, the middle class pupils had succeeded in retaining intact their historic advantages over the working class pupils. Jencks (1973) argued that for the lower class the inequalities of the parents had become more or less those of the children. Caldwell indicated that parents' deficits had tended to generate children's deficits.

Some of the research studies reviewed above have tended to place emphasis on school effects, others on home effects and some others on both as the major contributory factors to performances. Banks and Finlayson for example were inclined to attribute level of performance to school effects. Whereas, Halsey and Marsden (1962), Douglas, Plowden, Peaker and Coleman and Newson placed emphasis on home effects. The uncertainty of the knowledge of the effect of environmental factors on learning has made it difficult to devise relevant policies for the improvement of educational chances. Halsey (1972) reported that egalitarian policies had failed. Some research studies reviewed below, have also indicated that the learning disparity has tended to be more severe with deprived black pupils than with the deprived white pupils.

1.2 THE MEASURED DIFFERENCES BETWEEN BLACK AND WHITE PUPILS ON TEST SCORES

Coleman (1966) and Shuey (1966) reviewed IQ differences between black and white pupils in the USA and concluded that on average the blacks scored 15 points lower than the whites. Little et al., and Jenson also reported that the difference was 15 points. Houghton (1968) and McFie and Thompson (1970) reported that the differences were significant. Pidgeon (1970) reported on the other hand that using non verbal tests the blacks scores were higher than the whites in South Africa. Vernon rejected the 15 points discrepancy evidence on statistical grounds. Blain (1969), Payne (1969) and Haynes (1971) reported that non-verbal tests were not culturally free. Bhatnagan (1970) argued that intelligence tests were not unbiased between social groups. Cavalli-Storza (1970) stated that tests were not independent of environment. Goodman (1964), Tulkin (1968), William (1973) and Jencks (1973) rejected the validity of intelligence tests between social groups. Butcher (1968), Eysenck (1971), Jencks (1973) and Nuttal (1972) criticised the validity of intelligence test scales on their unidimensionality. Some of the existing test scales such as the Standford-Binet, the Wechsler Intelligence Scale and the Peabody Picture Voculary Test which had been standardised with the results obtained on white children were bound, according to some researchers, to have limitations when used with black children. Besides the reported cognitive differences between the blacks and the whites Jensen argued that the white children were genetically superior to the black children. Gordon (1970) stated Jensen's alleged genetic difference was value judgement based largely on speculation in inferences from disparate body of empirical data.

In the preceding sections some attempt has been made to review research studies on factors which influence educational opportunities. Many of the research studies reported already have tended to suggest the influence of genetic factors and others have argued that environment appeared to be crucial with school, home and neighbourhood, playing an important part. Discussions have been extended to appraise the nature of the differences between black and white pupils in cognitive test scores. The evidence advanced so far is insufficient to develop a vigorous theory of educational opportunity. The analyses of how each of the alleged factors have influenced attainment have not been made clear. Some of the researchers have defined learning narrowly and Butcher suggested widening the concept and constructing new types of measures. It appears from the above evidence that more research will be needed both on the content and on the context of

15

learning in order to improve and develop learning
theories. The review of compensatory education which
follows will highlight the increased need for
contextual studies of learning processes.

1.3   A REVIEW OF COMPENSATORY EDUCATION

The concept of compensatory education relies mainly on
the phenotypically induced as opposed to genotypically
induced traits. It relies in effect on the phenotypic
model of learning deficits. Jencks' and Halsey's
account of the limited role of education has rekindled
interest in the instrumental properties of nature and
nurture with respect to educational performance.

Historically, compensatory education has been linked
with the Headstart programmes in the USA. Clough
(1972) reported that President Johnson's commitment to
the war on poverty led to the Economic Opportunity Act
of 1964 which gave rise to the public funding of major
compensatory programmes in the USA. Sprehe et al.,
(1969) reported that besides the Headstart programmes,
Title I and Upward Bound constituted other forms of
compensatory programmes.

The Headstart was an intervention programme aimed at
preventing developmental deficits by the improvement of
academic, health and social service support. It began
as a pilot programme in 1965 under the auspices of the
office of the Economic Opportunity (OEO). The
programme ran for eight weeks with the initial enrolment of 500,000 children of pre-school age. Sub-
sequently it became a full-year programme. In 1967 the
programme ran in 13,000 local centres with varied
emphasis. The 1969 budget was 330 million dollars.

The Title I programme arose out of the Elementary and
Secondary Education Act launched in 1966. It was set
up to overcome educational deprivation associated with
poverty and race by providing medical care, dental
treatment, a lunch programme, teacher training,
diagnostic service, class room construction and

16

extended school day or year-round service. Funds were allocated by application to meet the needs of the pre-school, elementary and secondary school pupils. In practice, the main emphasis was placed on developing cognitive skills of reading, mathematics and the language of pupils, in the elementary schools. Sprehe et al. (1969) reported that Title I was the largest compensatory education programme of the OEO in 1966, with 215 educational institutions from 50 states taking part and covering 20,000 pupils in the initial programme. It started as an experimental Summer project and indicated that a pre-college experience for 'disadvantaged' children had some promise of success. In 1969 the cost of enrolment was 31 million dollars.

The Upward Bound project also aimed at developing cognitive skills. The treatment took the form of intensive Summer and after school contact in tutorials, enrichment activities and meetings. There were some similarities between the three projects but the commissioning of the 'Westinghouse' study by OEO in 1968 made the Headstart project more commonly associated with compensatory education.

In the UK some form of compensatory programme was attempted when the Schools Council gave financial support to the Department of Education, University College of Swansea in 1967 to carry out research and to develop projects for four and a half years. The aims were to provide screening techniques to enable children in need of compensatory education to be identified at an early age and to make longitudinal studies of infant school children in deprived areas with respect to emotional development and schooling and also to develop language materials which could be used in helping culturally deprived pupils at the infant school age. Gahagan and Gahagan (1970) reported on other exper-imental studies undertaken in the UK. Clough (1972) gave some account of similar projects in Australia and Israel. These accounts indicated the variability of these programmes with respect to method of experiment, selection procedure, organisation and objectives. These variations made comparative analyses problematic.

17

The Westinghouse evaluation of the Headstart project

The OEO commissioned researchers to provide objective
evidence on the consequences of the programmes during
1968 and 1969 with respect to their psychological and
intellectual impact on the pupils. Sprehe reported
that before this time, continuing systematic programmes
of evaluation did not exist. The researchers did not
have the opportunity to conduct longitudinal assessment
studies. The OEO commission was in effect an ex-post
facto evaluation study. This was a major weakness of
the exercise. This evaluation study became known as
the 'Westinghouse' study.

The researchers studied 31 Headstart programmes.
Seventeen programmes used control groups and before and
after designs, and fourteen programmes used before and
after design without control groups. A random assign-
ment of the pupils was exceptional and this necessitated caution in drawing conclusions about purported
effects. The data source covered documents, bulletin
studies, reports, curriculum, teachers, parents,
follow-up, language, cognitive development, motivation
and special problems.

The sample size was 1,980 pupils drawn from 104
Headstart centres and matched for age, sex, race and
kindergarten attendance. The pupils comprised the
first, second and third grades. These were matched
with the non-participating pupils. The socio-economic
status (SES) of the two groups were rendered comparable
by the use of covariance technique. Test batteries of
mental aptitude, scholastic achievement and attitudes
were administered to the two groups. This was supplemented with interviewing data obtained on the pupils,
parents and officials of the Headstart centres. The
teachers of the two groups completed rating forms on
learning. Covariance technique was used for the
analysis.

On the basis of the above study design, the
Westinghouse study reported that language development
was found not to be significant between the Headstart

subjects and their counterparts for the Summer
programmes. On the full-year programmes, two of the
sub-tests favoured the Headstart pupils. The Illinois
Test of Psycholinguistic Abilities was used. On the
readiness to enter school the Headstart pupils on the
full-year programmes achieved significantly higher
results than the control group. The Metropolitan
Readiness Test was used. On cognitive gains, significant differences between the Headstart and the control
group on the standard achievement tests were not
reported. On the affective gains, the Headstart pupils
from both the full-year and the Summer programmes did
not score significantly higher than the controls at any
of the three levels on measures of self-concept, desire
for achievement and attitude to school or to parents.

The national sample result showed few cases with
significant differences on a battery of six different
mental ability tests. A fading-out or a levelling-off
effect was reported and the long term effect was
slight. The majority of the significant programmes
reported adopted some form of planning.

The Title I programmes were analysed on the basis of
reading test scores from 1967 to 1968 obtained on
38,500 pupils drawn from 22 cities. Control groups
were not reported. The findings indicated that
improvement in reading and mathematics occurred, but at
a non-significant level. The drop-out rate decreased
by 5% and the attendance rate increased. The main
weaknesses of the study were biased sampling, non-
comparable data and the absence of control groups.

Granger et al. (1969) concluded that the Westinghouse
study of Headstart programmes showed that the impact on
pre-school learning was little. This conclusion
generated mixed reactions and criticisms of the
research design which gave added impetus to the
author's research.

Hawkridge, Chalupsky and Robert (1968) argued that
the evaluation design had a number of weaknesses. The
researchers adopted a 'black-box' strategy of design

19

by structuring observations to the input and output points. This did leave out the effects of the intervening and of the mediating factors on the pupils. The design was not sharp enough in detecting delayed maturation and interaction effects. Some critics indicated the difficulties associated with separating treatment effects from maturation ones. Smith and Bissell (1970) rejected the study on its ex-post design, sampling bias and in lumping all the programmes together in the study. Sprehe et al. (1969) criticised the classification and specification methods in that the Headstart centres were hetrogeneous and to lump them together for the purposes of analysis masked important differences.

Kagan (1969) stated that the method used did produce inadequate evidence and illogical conclusions. The design method was not sharp enough to compensate for the absence of pre-test and control groups, to isolate the impact of parents, neighbourhood, schools and teachers, to measure Hawthorne special attention and diffusion effects and to assess the test - retest, regression and cue effects.

It is possible for example, for a subject's observed scores to appear to be higher on a second test without any increase in knowledge or learning. In a pre-school programme, adults will tend to play a greater role than in programmes designed for older pupils. These factors were not taken into consideration. Scriven (1967) described the evaluation design as summative as against being formative. Sprehe et al. (1969) said that it was descriptive with low appraisal standard. Campbell and Erlebacher (1970) argued that the ex post facto evaluation method gave rise to systematic bias. Cicenelli et al. (1969) thought this was the most serious weakness in the Westinghouse evaluation study and this method of evaluation was not consistent with covariance analysis.

On the technology of testing Bereiter argued that the pre-school test scales for measuring cognitive skills were very limited. Rohwer (1971) suggested that early

20

childhood could not constitute a stable testing and learning period. Bereiter doubted Piaget's assumptions that children tended to regress to a similar stage of mental development at six years of age.

Zimiles (1970) reported that tests provided indirect information on cognitive processes mediating the child's current intellectual functioning and that using pre - post test evaluation methods yielded only measures of accomplishment without measures of mediating cognitive processes. Clough reported that the researchers used the S-B tests and the tests of specific cognitic skills were not uncommon. Clough argued that the tests of achievement while relatively common, were on so many different batteries that comparison was virtually impossible. Bereiter and Englemann rejected the reliability of the IQ gains since some programme children were reported to have high achievement gains but low IQ scores. In the author's research experience, this may not necessarily be inconsistent since an environmentally induced threshold effect can boost the initial low score substantially as a result of compensatory treatment.

Palmer said that the crucial factor of the treatment method was the interpersonal relationship. This was difficult to evaluate. Jensen (1969)said that the compensatory programmes failed because learning symptoms were more amenable to genetic than to environmental treatment, and that compensatory education represented a partial treatment of a concomitant factor. Crow (1969), Deutsch (1969), Hunt (1969) and Kagan (1969) rejected Jensen's interpretation. Clough discredited the assumptions of the programmes. Bereiter and Engelmann doubted the efficiency of the verbally rich middle class setting being appropriate for compensating the culturally and linguistically deprived child. Hunt (1969(a) and 1969(b)) and Elkind (1969) thought that the age of intervention was the main factor affecting the results. The different levels of the results of the compensatory education programmes are reported below.

21

Gordon (1969) reported that after one year of compensatory programme, significant differences in overall intelligence quotient, sensory co-ordination and social skills were found in favour of the experimental groups. Gordon concluded that a relatively untrained personnel would produce gains. Karnes et al. (1970), McConnell Horton and Smith (1969) found that after one year, the experimental groups made significantly larger gains on all tests. Palmer (1969), who arranged for his two year subjects to attend a centre for two hours per week for eight months, reported that the experimental group performed better than the control group on the Cattell intelligence test, Illinois test of Psycholinguistic Abilities scores, and on the Merrill-Palmer language and conceptual development test. Schaefer's experimental units performed better than the control ones. Weikart (1967), Weikart and Radin (1964) who adapted their programme over a period of several years reported that the experimental group gained 15 points on the Binet Scale while the control group gained three points. This difference had tended to disappear when the children entered school. The initial effect reported was that the control group showed rapid rise while the experimental group dropped slightly and further schooling resulted in a rise in scores of the experimental group on reading readiness and achievement tests.

The Blank and Solomon (1968) programme focussing on language development resulted in the experimental group gaining significantly more than the control group by 14.5 points. This study supports Bereiter and Engelmann's hypothesis that language development and cognitive gains are positively associated. The study by Dawe (1942) of institutional children using language development programme in small groups, showed that the experimental group gained 14.2 points on the Binet scale while the control group experienced a small loss of two points. The two groups showed significant gains on measures of vocabulary. But the differences between the groups favoured the experimental groups. The experimental group in the study received 50 hours of training in over eight months period. The control and

the experimental groups attended pre-schools. The
school programme included picture, discussion, stories,
excursion and concept development. The IQ gain
reported by Dawe compared favourable with the more
focussed studies, suggesting that the drill methods of
Bereitor and Engelmann might have been unnecessary.

Moffitt and Nurcombe (1970), Moffitt, Nurcombe,
Passmore and McNeilly (1971) used a modified Bereiter
and Engelmann programme, a traditional programme with
aboriginal and European pre-school population in New
South Wales, Australia. More gains were made on the
Bereiter and Engelmann treatment than on the traditional treatment. The difference was reported to be
significant. In Israel, Smilansky and Smilansky (1970)
reported that the traditional kindergarten was
inappropriate for intervention work. Consequently the
researchers developed more activity based programmes
with focus on language, cognitive and motivational
skills judged against the criterion of their ability to
learn when the child entered school. The earlier
reports of the Smilansky work in 1964, indicated that
attendance at the experimental kindergarten was
associated with IQ gains of 10 points over the
attendance of the ordinary kindergartens. The
researchers indicated that the appropriate organisational units needed and demanded mixed age groups and
several teachers with democratic but hierachical
sharing of authority. The teachers were expected to
have effective knowledge of the pupils.

In the USA Deutsch (1965, 1967) and Goldskin (1965)
carried out intervention research aimed at developing
cognitive and learning skills. The period of intervention was five years. Many of the traditional
activities were retained but gains related to the
development of vocabulary, auditory training, visual
discrimination and attitude to learning were given
greater emphasis. The experimental and the control
group scored an IQ of 99 on S-B at entry. After one
year the experimental group scores rose to 102 while
the control group scores fell to 93. After a further
year the scores were 104 and 92 respectively. Other

tests of intelligence and achievement favoured the experimental group. Van de Reit and Van de Reit (1968) used two control groups of traditional kindergarten and non-attendance in their experiment. At the end of the kindergarten year the experimental group scored 104 points while the traditional group scored 90 points. The non-attendance group scored 83. The experimental group was superior significantly to the traditional groups on a number of other measures. The traditional group was significantly better than the non-attendance group on about half the measures. After one year of school attendance, the experimental group was still superior on the S-B scores. On the other hand, Clough reporting on the supplementary language experiment on cognitive development of children attending kindergarten in low SES area found that although seven of the eight tests favoured the experimental group, yet in none of the cases was the difference between the groups significant. In the UK Gahagan and Gahagan (1970) showed that the mean score of the experimental group was superior to that of the control group on all tests except on one of the two tests of creativity. The significant difference in language and social skills favoured the experimental group.

The gains made were reported to fade out over time. Gray (1969) and Gray and Klaus (1966 and 1970) who carried out intervention programmes with varying levels of treatment reported that the excess of gains made by the experimental group over the control group of nine points in two and a half years, decreased in subsequent years. McCandles and Spicker (1967), Weikart, Kamii and Radin (1964), and Clough (1972) concluded that persistence of gains did not appear to hold. The main characteristics of the compensatory programmes, the method used, the levels of treatment applied and the results obtained are examined critically below.

Gray and Miller (1967) reported, that most of the programme could be classified into specific or overall intervention. Some of these programmes used different methods of stimulation involving the younger age groups on the notion of the effect of early intervention.

Nixon (1969), Bloom (1964) and Deutsch (1967) reported that the younger ones were more sensitive to treatment and they did not suffer the effect of cumulative deficits. This position can be criticised on methodological grounds since the problem of adult effect and measurement are associated with early intervention. In the USA selection criterion discriminated in favour of the minority, racial and working class groups, and the pre-school and kindergarten programmes were favoured. There is an overlapping of the pre-school and kindergarten education in both the United Kingdom and Australia. But in the USA pre-school has tended to precede kindergarten education and the latter included children in the first year of elementary school.

Rusk (1967) reported that many of the Headstart programmes ran for only six weeks, but Gray and Klaus (1970) indicated that other programmes retained their subjects for up to three years. The organisational structure of most of the programmes involved an adult – child ratio of about five to one. Blank and Solomon (1968) used a one to one ratio. The area of focus varied also. For example some programmes stressed language development as a major treatment factor such as Bereiter and Engelmann (1966), as well as the Blank and Solomon (1968) programmes. Others stressed the need for the child to develop positive self-concept, greater attention span, positive attitude to achievement, creative, and social relations skills. Smilansky and Smilansky (1970) attempted to develop school orientated skills and Weikart (1969) aimed at developing more general skills. Some programmes were diagnostic and others like Deutsch (1968) and Karner et al. (1970) were based directly on the child's weaknesses.

Keliher (1969) and Gordon (1969) used parents as teachers for their own children after some form of preliminary training and with varying degrees of continuing support. Painter (1969) and Schaefer (1969) tutored the children in their own homes. Caldwell (1967), McConnell, Horton and Smith (1969) and Robinson (1969) used a tutorial system at day care centres while Palmer (1969) made shorter visits to centres. The Caldwell day care programme operated for up to twelve hours per day and five days a week, while Palmer centre visits involved only two hours of tutoring per week. Painter (1969) and Schaefer ran their programmes for one hour per day on a five day week and on a ratio of one to one. These programme variations with respect to selection, objective, maturation, operational design made it difficult to evaluate and contrast the results. Osborn (1968) and Sontag, Sella and Thorndike (1969) stated that the quasi-heterogeneity of these programmes made it necessary to interpret the evidence of compensatory studies with caution. The case studies reported below will highlight the basic characteristics and weaknesses discussed already.

TWO CASES AND THEIR IMPLICATIONS

Case 1

Programme title. Bereiter - Engelmann Academic Pre-School Programme originated at the Institute for Research on Exceptional Children, University of Illinois.

Maturation level of target population. From pre-school to junior school.

Objective. To teach language, reading and arithmetic skills to a low SES group of mostly negro pupils.

Operational design. Classes ran for two hours daily, for five days a week, for one academic year. The pupil-teacher ratio was 5.1. Teaching was confined to a highly structured small group with emphasis on cognitive growth and not on socio-emotional development. Teachers were selected and trained in the methods. Parents were involved where possible and control groups were not used in the first year of the programme.

26

Results. Rusk (1969), reported that the result was positive. The replication study by Rusk showed that after six weeks of Summer operation, the academically orientated projects were more positive than the socially orientated ones.

Implication. Sprehe et al. (1969) said that the results confirmed the views of the cognitive school that early intellectual stimulation would develop academic potential. The evidence obtained indicated that the more the disadvantage the greater the potential for gains ceteris paribus.

Case 2

Programme title. The Early Training Project at Peabody College.

Maturation level of target population. Pre-school age.

Objective. To prevent handicaps which might militate against school programme.

Operational design. Some emphasis was placed on the positive attitudes and aptitudes to achievement in the school. Perceptual, language development and concept formation were nurtured. Home visits were made by trained workers.

Pupils were randomly selected into two experimental groups and two control groups. One control group was local and the other was non-local. One experimental group practiced for three Summers and another for two. Four standardised ability tests were administered for the cognitive effects and four tests of affective domain were administered.

Results. Success in changing motivation and attitude remained uncertain. The aptitude tests showed significant gains in favour of the experimental groups. The diffusion and the maturation effects were not significant. Granger's statement of the likelihood of significant effect with a year-round programme was not confirmed.

Implications. The comparison between the combined averages of the experimental and the control groups did tend to influence the significant test.

Sprehe stated that the above case studies which were linked with institutions of higher learning were a few of the studies with improved methods of design. It was reported also that despite the quasi-improvement on the methodology, the studies did not establish conclusively any consistency in achieving significant gains in both the cognitive and affective measures readily. Sprehe stated further that these research designs did not establish the criteria for programme design, data collection and data analysis.

It appears from the preceding analysis that the main weaknesses of the compensatory programmes were the level of methodological design, the choice of age of intervention, of the validity of the measuring instruments and the absence of the theory of deprivation. Clough, Smith and Bissell, Rohwer and Bereiter and Engelmann stated that these weaknesses limited the results. Clough observed that the increase in intelligence scores, for example, might not have been accompanied by increase in achievement skills although there was a strong tendency for this to occur. One factor being that the predictive power of scores obtained after intervention programmes have not been established to the same extent that the results obtained under ordinary conditions have been validated. Also, although some of the more structured programmes with the specific treatment areas have tended to prove more effective, the intelligence tests which were used as the main independent variable cannot discriminate systematically between attainment and ability since intelligence tended to vary concomitantly with attainment.

Gahagan (1970) and Little (1973) reported findings in which a low teacher - pupil ratio generated small effect on learning. This conflicts with the implicit

assumption of associating increased learning with a
high ratio of teacher - pupil on which most of the
compensatory programme depended. The small part played
by training coupled with the non-randomisation in the
sampling constituted a major limitation. Sprehe argued
that in social sciences, the difficulty of meeting, the
randomisation criterion constituted a serious problem.
In social action programmes the experimental demands of
random selection and control conflicted always with
administrative and moral considerations according to
Sprehe. The study of deprived pupils as a group has
tended to limit the potential for inferences.

The design of the author's research has been
influenced to a certain extent by the evidence of the
methodological weaknesses discussed already. For
example, the author's research ran for six years and
this rendered it feasible to replicate the experiment
and to compare the results. The first and second
years were used as pilot and control studies respectively. Training constituted an important part of the
design thus allowing for the standardisation and the
rationalisation of the processes. A system of planned
analysis and evaluation was built into the research
programmes and retained throughout the six years.
This was a major departure from some of the Headstart
designs. The evaluation system included pilot and
control studies, before and after testing, recording,
interviewing, sociometric and social adjustment
studies. Parents, teachers, pupils and group leaders
provided additional data.

2 Method

2.1 DESCRIPTION OF THE STUDY

The programme title: an action research of
compensatory education programmes.

The subjects and sample size. A total of 383 pupils
with learning difficulties as defined by the schools,
who were either in their last year of primary, or first
year of secondary schooling were selected by the
schools to take part in the programmes. For details
see Table 2.1 below. The majority of the pupils were
drawn from the low socio-economic status group and were
on average nine years old.

The objectives

   To raise the test quotient (IQ) of the subjects.
   To improve English and mathematics achievement.
   To evaluate the effect of the treatment.
   To develop some theory of educational deprivation.

Hypothesis

To test the strength of the gains made by the subjects,
if any, in English, mathematics and social skills.

2.2 THE OPERATIONAL DESIGN

There were two thirty minute breaks per day, one in the
morning and the other in the afternoon. Learning of
English, mathematics and social skills took place
during the group work sessions in particular. The
other sessions were spent in the workshop or on
educational study visits, talks, stories, film shows,
music and discussions. The activities during the workshops were directed to developing a common experience
and relating the experience to learning skills. Pupils

Table 2.1

Teacher - pupil ratio

Participants Programme Years	Number of Pupils	Teachers		Number of participating schools	Teacher - pupil ratio excluding the leaders
		Leaders	Supervisors		
1970	28	4	3	3	1:9
1971	152	16	14	26	1:12
1972	45	6	6	6	1:7
1973	70	10	4	5	1:17
1974	54	9	3	13	1:21
1976	14	2	1	3	1:14
					Average ratio
Total	383	47	31	56	1:12

Table 2.2

The operational structure of the programme

Sessions / Days	Morning session		Break	Afternoon session	
	09.00–09.30	09.30–12.00	12.00–13.30	13.30–15.30	15.30–17.00
MONDAY		Group work	L	Outing and/or workshop	
TUESDAY	Preparation session for supervisors and leaders at the project centre	Outing and/or workshop	U	Group work	Training session for supervisors and leaders at the project centre
WEDNESDAY		Group work	N	Outing and/or workshop	
THURSDAY		Outing and/or workshop	C	Group work	
FRIDAY		Group work	H	Plenary session	

were randomly assigned to the study groups of about
eight. A supervisor and one or two leaders were
responsible for each group. The leaders engaged the
pupils in learning and the supervisors facilitated the
learning and acted as consultants. As a vehicle for
work, each group member was given support and friendship and nurtured to develop a repertoire of responses.
Pupils were stimulated to practice articulating their
thoughts and individual interest was encouraged with
support from the leaders and supervisors. English,
mathematics and social skills were the main subjects on
which the evaluation of performance was based.

The instruments used. Mathematics attainment tests A
and B, picture test, reading tests AD and BD, NFER,
Holborn Reading Scale, Bristol Social Adjustment Guides
and a sociometric test developed by Button (1972) were
used. The 1970 study was a pilot one, the 1971 was a
control study and the 1972, 1973, 1974 and 1976 were
experimental. Before and after interviews and
questionnaires were administered to supplement the
data. Personal background forms were used in all the
programmes. Since it was not possible to secure reading and mathematics tests suitable for all the pupils
because of their wide age range, some selection of
tests which covered the mean age of the subjects was
made. Dr Sumner of the NFER and Dr Little of the
former Community Relations Commission gave some useful
advice on the selection of the tests.

The learning aids. School and library books, The
Science Research Associate Reading Laboratory and
Mathematics Kit, Longman Reading Rootes, films and
tapes were used.

The scoring. The tests were marked by the teachers and
the scores were scaled to its IQ equivalent. Correc-
tions were made in scoring each pupil, to take account
of age.

The statistical tools used. Mean, standard deviation,
frequency distribution, percentages, regression,
correlation coefficients and covariance tables were

computed.   F-test and t-test were also used.

The quasi-experimental design

Years	Programme duration	Treatment type	Design type
1970	One week	I Xo I	Pilot group
1971	Three weeks	I Xo I T	Control group
1972	Three weeks	I T S X: I T C S	Experimental group
1973	Three weeks	I T X: I T	Experimental group
1974	Three weeks	I T X: I T S	Experimental group
1976	One week	I Xo I T	Experimental group

Key
```
I   = interviewing
Xo  = treatment with discovery method
X:  = treatment with discovery method and SRA
T   = testing
C   = child study
S   = sociometric test
```

The data sources for evaluating the treatment effect.
The sources of data were test scores, child study,
Sociometric Study, interviewing records, teachers and
leaders reports, parents, schools and pupils follow up
studies and recording.

The Reasearch Consultant.   Dr Patrick Quinn of
Tavistock Institute of Human Relations was the
Consultant in the 1970 and 1971 projects.

The research staff.   There were three staff in the 1970
and 1971 projects; two staff in the 1972, 1973, 1974
and 1976 projects and of these the author was appointed
with special responsibility for the research aspect of
the projects.

The learning method.   The child centred, group learning
and discovery method of learning processes were used.
The discovery method was designed to motivate the
pupils to learn the specific cognitive and affective
skills.   This method involved the attempt to relate

34

pupil learning to programmed experience through creative exposure and positive stimulation. The organisation was flexible and informal. The content level and direction of learning were related to the age, ability level, and interest points of the pupils. For example data on pupils difficulties during the pre-tests was used as the starting point for subsequent exploration and development and pupils were encouraged to utilize previous experience. Specific learning areas were developed in the morning and the afternoon was used in making visits related to the morning programme. The group members were given choice and knowledge of results was fed back to the groups. The teachers were provided with some knowledge of the ability, emotions and social readiness of their pupils and the training programme was used in nurturing corporate spirit.

2.3   THE TRAINING ACTIVITY

Systematic induction programmes, regular training sessions and follow-up seminars were run for the members of the team. Learning and discovery method, curriculum development and sensitivity skills were some of the areas covered in the training. Sessions were devoted to exploring the level of experience, increasing insight, standardising operations and developing learning strategies. These sessions were held both before and after each day. For further details see Table 2.2. The researchers adopted questioning and diagnostic roles during the training aimed at generating objective data for subsequent exploration. Sessions were run also on the learning aids and instruments that were used. The training emphasis was placed on learning processes, project objectives and therapeutic use of activities for self-development and group interaction. The trainees were encouraged to be informal, to base operations on the needs of the pupils and to use christian names with the pupils. The seminars were devoted to the study of overt behaviour, and the sensitivity skills offered aimed at helping the trainees to be objective when interpreting the manifest behaviour of the pupils and to recognise signs. Concept such as group norms, controls and teachers' roles were highlighted in the training.

The training material was derived from the author's work on job analysis, job description and job specification. This study provided some basis for the selection and training of teachers and leaders. It included also result areas, conflict points and styles of command. It indicated the importance of interpreting knowledge with skills.

The teachers learned methods of arousing pupils commitment to learning through motivation. The learning was seen in terms of developing the pupils skills in perception, sufficient to internalise external stimuli, through the processes of assimilation, accommodation and adaptation. The teachers were helped to reflect critically on the patterns of group interactions, in order to achieve a balance between pupil's excitement on the one hand, and learning on the other, or between affective or instrumental behaviour. The teachers recognised the constraints of curriculum orientation, group norms and activity setting on learning and utilized this knowledge in widening pupils' options and initiative.

In one of the 1972 training sessions, taken by Mr Spink of the Tavistock Institute of Human Relations, the main areas covered were tasks, roles and attitudes. The teachers learned to develop their own control mechanism through the identification and classification of tasks and roles, the control of socio-task interaction and the establishment of unified boundaries between task and roles. Feelings were seen to give vital clues about what went on. The teachers were aware of the complex demands that could be made on people in a training group. Other factors examined in the training included the way that attitude, and personality might influence learning. Finally, the teachers saw themselves as members of a team using discovery method, social skills and a flexible approach to encourage the pupils to explore.

The selection of schools, pupils, teachers and leaders

Letters were sent to all the junior schools in each
locality. The head teachers were asked to select
pupils on the basis of low cognitive performance
equivalent to grade C stream. Pupils were accepted on
the basis of nominations from schools. More pupils
wanted to enrol than the available number of places.

In the 1970, 1971 and 1972 studies, a high proportion
of the pupils had an overseas background. In the 1973
and 1974 studies all the pupils were English but the
1976 study included four West Indian pupils.

Teachers and leaders were selected mainly from the
participating schools. These teachers and leaders
expressed favourable attitudes to the project and their
motivational factor tended to be influenced more by
interest than by financial considerations. This meant
in practise, the desire to help the pupils.

The professional status of the research study

The Inner London Education Authority school inspectors
involved in sanctioning the study demanded and approved
both the teaching method to be used and the status of
the project director. In Surrey emphasis for approval
was placed on recruiting qualified teachers. All the
sponsors asked for the reports and for the statement of
income and expenses of each project.

3 Results

3.1 THE CHARACTERISTICS OF THE PARTICIPANTS

The data for the analysis below were obtained from the test scores, personal background study, interviews, recordings, child study, sociometric study, teachers' reports, parents, schools, and pupils follow-up studies. The personal background study showed that the majority of the parents were employed in manual and unskilled jobs; most of the families had four or more children per family; some of these families lived in houses or in flats with multiple occupations and with inadequate toilet facilities; and Sunday school attendance was higher amongst the immigrant pupils than with the English ones. Some of the immigrant pupils were less able to read and write formal English than the English pupils and communication between schools and homes was found to be more limited for the immigrant parents than for the English ones. The participation in extra-school activities by the immigrant pupils was less than the participation by other pupils. Although evidence of installed television was recorded, that of books was not.

The three London programmes contained a high proportion of pupils with overseas background. For example, in the 1970 project 20 of the 28 pupils accepted were of Jamaican parents. Six of these were of Irish and two were of English parents. The Nigerian, Italian, Greek and Mauritian pupils who were selected failed to enrol. One explanation given was that the parents had forgotten the dates of the project. The basic characteristics were therefore a high percentage of working parents, large families, and a high proportion of immigrant pupils. The family size was on average 6.1. The pupils were aged on average 8.8 years. About 73% of the fathers and 57% of the mothers were fully employed. The 28 pupils who were selected from three schools comprised 17 girls and 11 boys. In one of the schools 70% of the pupils came from overseas with about 90% of these pupils in one class. The pupils were reported to be recent arrivals to England after long periods of separation from their natural parents. The above picture was typical of the 1971 and 1972 projects. The schools did not provide data on the attitude, aptitude, behaviour and friendship link of the pupils. Therefore the interpretation of the evidence was based mainly on the experience of the projects.

The analysis of the study indicates that the attitude of the teachers and leaders to the pupils, the learning method used and the activity setting, affected what went on. The effect was more expressive and less cognitive. Some of the pupils progressed from being shy, reticent and withdrawn to becoming active, helpful and cheerful. The attachment to group activities tended to be influenced more by friendship and interest considerations than by the actual activity itself. The group processes helped the pupils to explore new levels of experience and task achievement tended to be more affective and less instrumental. Some of the pupils displayed unusual levels of excitement. The follow-up study made on parents and schools indicated the project had some positive effect on the pupils. Some parents reported that their children had asked them for help in joining the local library after participating in the project. Some teachers reported on the evidence of improved social behaviour and all the pupils wished for a repeat of similar projects in their next school holiday.

Some of the problems experienced in the 1970 project included the funding of the project, the organising of dinners and the transporting of the pupils and anxiety on the part of some parents about their children being selected for the project. For example, some of these parents thought that the selecting of their children was part of the process of sending them to special schools. Experimentally, the design and duration of the 1970 project did not allow for the application of sophisticated statistical analysis: the design of control and experimental groups and the administration of before and after tests were left out.

Therefore, in judging the pupils' responses to the project, it was thought that if the participating parents held more favourable attitudes to the project than the non-participating ones, then this was bound to have some positive effect on their children. Some evidence of these differences has been recorded already. Of the participating pupils, the boys, especially the older ones have tended to be less involved with the group processes than the girls. The girls have tended to band together at break time and relationships between the sexes did not appear to be fluid.

The evidence of the 1970 study indicated that the low socio-economic status of the parents, large family size, overcrowding, low level of reading and writing attainment of the pupils, low involvement of the pupils in extra-school activities, limited educational exper- ience, inadequate day care in the area, the limited communication between teachers and the parents and limited maternal and emotional satisfaction may be associated with the pupils low levels of school performance. This evidence appears to highlight some of the accounts given by Plowden (1967) and Douglas (1964) as stated already in the review of the literature. The two studies showed negative effects of family size on school performance in particular. The experience of this pilot study provided the author with a relevant methodological basis for the design of the 1971 control study and the 1972, 1973, 1974 and 1976 experimental studies.

The 1971 project ran for three weeks and was designed as a control experiment. A total of 14 teachers, 16 leaders and 162 pupils took part. The pupils were selected from 26 local schools. The teachers were made up of seven student teachers, six graduates and one trained teacher with some years of teaching experience. The mean age of the teachers was 23 years. Three of these teachers were between 35 and 40 years of age.

The family size of the teachers was less than four and hence small.

Of the 16 leaders, there were more girls than boys. The boys tended to be older than the girls. The mean age of the leaders was 15.5 and the family size was larger than that of the teachers. The mean age difference between the leaders and the supervisors was seven years. The pupils came from large families and their parents were manually employed.

In 1972 the personnel structure included 45 pupils, six teachers, and six senior pupils. The pupils were drawn from six schools with family size 4.7. The parents of these pupils did unskilled jobs. Of the six leaders, two had experience of similar projects. All the six teachers were trained and qualified with two or more years of experience. The mean age of the teachers was 32 years and their formal qualifications included degrees, diplomas and certificates. The teachers were on average more qualified and experienced in 1972 than in the other years. The 1972, 1973, 1974 and 1976 projects were designed as experimental studies.

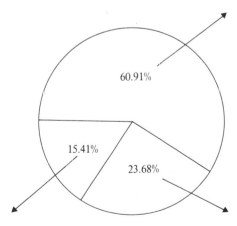

consanguine family type with two of the parents being wholly employed in unskilled jobs

60.91%

15.41%

23.68%

consanguine family type with one parent usually an unemployed mother

consanguine family type with one of the parents being wholly employed in unskilled jobs

Figure 3.1 The typology of the families

The main characteristics of the parents of the pupils
in the 1972 study included a high level of employment,
large family size and low involvement of the parents
with the schools attended by their children. The one
parent family household, in which the only adult member
present was the mother, was found to be higher with the
West Indians than with any other ethnic group. There
were six of such families in the 1972 study. For the
details see Figure 3.1 above.

The study of the pupils' subject preferences showed
that the boys disliked writing and reading and the
girls, especially the West Indian ones, disliked
physical exercise. One girl said she was too shy to
exhibit herself. Stories and reading tended to be
popular with the girls, while history and craft were
preferred by the boys. The differences in subject
preferences between the boys and the girls were
reflected only slightly in the test scores.

The personnel structure of the 1973 study included
70 pupils, four teachers and ten leaders. The average
number of children in the families of the pupils was
4.1 and the mean age was 8.95 years. The pupils were
classified by their schools as below average ability
and the majority of the pupils' parents did unskilled
jobs. Of the leaders, the mean age was 13.8 years,
family size 3.4 and most of them were in the B stream
grade.

The 1974 and 1976 studies participants were 78 pupils
from 16 schools, eleven leaders and three teachers.
The analysis of the personal background study of the
pupils who completed the forms showed that they were
low on verbal skills and SES of parents and high on
family size. The mean age was 8.27 years in 1974 and
9.71 years in 1976. The 1974 and 1976 studies like the
previous ones showed that the subjects were character-
ised by low potential for academic work, toleration
level, social skills and SES of parents but high
spontaneity, attention seeking, family size,
deprivation, overcrowding and unstimulating home.
These factors have been reported by other studies to be

associated with underfunctioning in schools. The pupils with low test scores in the project have tended also to be severely affected by those factors. The Plowdens stated in their report that low SES groups of children have tended to be held back from performing well in schools because of their home conditions. Some of the parents were recorded to be unemployed and those employed did unskilled jobs. In most of the families with jobs both parents were reported to be wholly employed. This picture was not dissimilar to the 1973 study. The children who were sponsored by the social services were found to be relatively more deprived than the others. Some of these were found to be subnormal on the IQ scale. These children and their families tended to make greater demands on the resources of the project.

The study of the pupils' aspirations revealed that the girls aspired to jobs in shops, teaching, nursing and hairdressing and boys preferred lorry driving, the police force and the services. The choices between the girls and boys were found to follow rather closely those of the parents. A high proportion recorded that they did not attend Sunday schools and church connection appeared to be weak especially with the older pupils. The girls' subject preferences were English, art and projects while the boys chose sports and games. Most of the boys in the study recorded having had some experience of week-end jobs such as car-cleaning, milk and paper rounds. The eleven leaders in the 1974 and 1976 studies were all girls aged, on average, 14.6 years with a high interest and motivation. Most of them came from small family units and their employed parents were in semi-skilled occupations.

The personal background study of the six programmes showed that the pupils in 1970, 1971, 1972, 1973, 1974 and 1976 were similar with respect to the SES of their parents. The pupils in 1970, 1971 and 1972 differed with respect to measured attainment. The mean scores in English and mathematics were higher in the last three than in the first three studies. More than 50% of the pupils who attended the 1970, 1971 and 1972

43

programmes received free school dinners, whereas in the 1973, 1974 and 1976 studies this was less than 33.5% but most of the pupils in all the projects tended to depend on the project dinner for their main meal. The evidence stated above provided the basis for the statistical analysis and comparative evaluations of the effects, if any, of the treatment.

3.2   ANALYSIS OF TEST SCORES

Table 3.1
The distribution of the English test* result in 1971

Standardised English Quotient	Frequency
Under 70	0
70 to under 80	28
80 to under 90	2
90 to under 100	0
100 to under 110	0
110 to under 120	0
Over 120	0

* Picture test

Table 3.1 shows that 93.3% of the pupils were in the 70 to 80 EQ range.

$\bar{x}_o$ = the mean score in English test of the group in 1971 was 73.77

S_{x_o} = the standard deviation was 3.59

The above scores have been transformed into 'English Quotient'. (EQ) equivalents with a mean of 100 and a standard deviation of 15. The 3.59 standard deviation in the English test score of the control group shows how the pupils clustered around the mean score of 73.77. It indicated also the degree of homogeneity of

44

the pupils with respect to their performance in English. Jensen and others have stipulated that a mean IQ score of 85 or more correlates strongly with academic functioning, while the mean IQ of 70 or under might indicate symptoms of subnormality. This comparison suggests therefore that the majority of the 1971 pupils with the mean EQ score of 73.77 have low levels of academic functioning. Since, according to Little, most of the severely disadvantaged West Indian pupils have been placed in special schools rather haphazardly, one would have expected those in the ordinary schools to be potentially capable of responding to learning stimulation. This did not appear to be the case with the pupils in the project. Table 3.1 above has shown that about 93.3% of the West Indian pupils have EQ scores of between 70 and 80.

Jencks (1973) reported that 67% of American children scored between 85 and 115 IQ. This comparison indicates the degree of the discrepancy between the West Indian pupils as a group and white pupils in academic functioning.

Table 3.2
The distribution of the English and mathematics tests in 1972

Class intervals	Before		After	
	x_1	y_1	x_2	y_2
Under 70	5	8	1	1
70 to under 80	11	7	12	8
80 to under 90	3	3	6	9
90 to under 100	2	3	2	3
100 to under 110	2	3	1	3
110 to under 120	1	0	1	0
Over 120	0	0	1	0

45

Table 3.2 shows that in English 63.3% and in mathematics 56.25% of pupils were in the 70–90 IQ range.

$\bar{x}_1$ = English test mean score of before treatment = 78.63, Sx_1 = 15.05

$\bar{y}_1$ = Mathematics test mean score of before treatment = 78.13, Sy_1 = 13.78, $rx_1 y_1$ =0.71

$\bar{x}_2$ = English test mean score of after treatment = 83.38, Sx_2 = 13.30

$\bar{y}_2$ = Mathematics test mean score of after treatment = 83.75, Sx_2 = 14.92, $rx_2 y_2$ =0.66

The high correlation coefficients of 0.71 and 0.66 suggest that the pupils scores in one subject tended to predict scores in the subsequent subject, but the percentages of the variance explained in the two instances were 50.41% for the before test and 43.56% for the after test. These values show the percentages of the linear relationship that can be explained in both the before and after test scores.

The pooled mean test scores for the West Indian pupils and the non West Indian pupils in English and mathematics were 76.24 and 77.85 as against 90.83 and 85.83 respectively. This suggests that the non West Indian pupils were superior to the West Indian pupils by 14.59 points in English and 7.98 points in mathematics tests. This gives a pooled mean discrepancy of 11.28. The non West Indian pupils included Nigerians, Indians, English and Jews. This result suggests that the West Indian pupils performed less well on attainment than the other pupils. The pooled mean scores of the West Indian pupils in the two subjects were 80.60 for the boys and 73.50 for the girls. This gives a discrepancy of 4.6% in favour of the boys. This indicates that the boys tended on average to perform better than the girls. This evidence conflicts with the NFER 1969 findings in which the girls were reported to score higher than the boys. This conflict may relfect differences in sampling. In the 1972 study the West Indian boys were on average older than the West Indian girls and the younger the age range the more unstable cognitive test scores would tend to be.

The combined mean scores of the Indian and the Nigerian pupils were higher than the combined mean scores of the West Indian and the English pupils in the two tests. This result conflicts with some of the reported evidence which had shown that English pupils performed better on cognitive test scores than the non English with the control of the parental SES. But this evidence supports the Tizard (1974) report on the evidence of the similarity of the mean IQ between different racial groups. This point cannot be over-stated since the above evidence is based on a small sample size.

3.3 TEST OF THE TREATMENT EFFECT IN 1972

Given the tabulated F-test of f_{23}^{23} for $\alpha = 0.05$, to be 4.28 and the computed F-test to be 2.262, the hypothesis that the $S_{x_1}^2 = S_{x_2}^2$ is accepted. This evidence indicates the likelihood of the treatment effect being significant. This then results in testing the hypothesis that the means of the before and after tests are not significantly different. Since the samples were correlated, Sandler's t-test for matched pairs was used. This resulted in gains in English being significant at 5% level. For the actual computation see Appendix 3. In the computation the mathematics gain was found to be significant. The mathematics gain was slightly higher than the gain in English by 0.87 points. The African and the Asian pupils as a group scored higher on average in mathematics than in English and their pooled mean scores in the two subjects was superior to the combined mean scores of the West Indian and the English pupils. This

47

suggests that some of the immigrant pupils experienced less difficulty in mathematics than the English pupils, while the English pupils experienced less difficulty in English than some of the immigrant pupils. Since the mathematics tests that were administered have been described as non-verbal and hence socio-culturally less biased than the English tests, this may suggest that the low scores by the pupils may reflect partly the bias of the testing instruments and partly the pupils' relative weaknesses in the two subjects. The deficiency in English allowing for the bias already stated, appears to affect the immigrant pupils more than the English pupils.

The mean difference between the 1971 and the 1972 scores in English was 4.38% in favour of the 1972 group. This indicates that the 1972 pupils were on average superior to the 1971 pupils on the English test scores. Since the two groups were similar with respect to ethnicity, age, SES and sex, it appears that the 1971 pupils were more deficient in English than the 1972 pupils.

The computation of the regression coefficients yield $bx_1y_1 = 0.65$ and $bx_2y_2 = 0.74$ for both the before and after test scores when regressing y on x. The positive coefficients in the two instances indicate that English and mathematics scores changed in the same direction. This suggests that pupils who obtained high scores in English were more likely to obtain high scores in mathematics. This degree of dependence between scores in English and in mathematics, indicated by the computation of the regression coefficient, has reinforced the earlier interpretation of the high degree of linearity in English and mathematics as shown by the correlation coefficient values of 0.71 and 0.66 reported already.

In 1973, 46 pupils took the before test in English and of these, only 19 pupils completed the after test. In the mathematics test the figures were before test 17 pupils and after test 8 pupils. This low response in mathematics tests limited the statistical value of

Table 3.3
The distribution of the test scores in
English and mathematics in 1973

Distribution	Before tests		After tests	
Intervals	x_1	y_1	x_2	y_2
Under 70	1	1	1	1
70 to under 80	3	1	2	0
80 to under 90	1	1	1	1
90 to under 100	0	4	1	4
100 to under 110	2	1	2	2
110 to under 120	1	0	1	0
Over 120	0	0	0	0

The above Table shows that 50% of pupils were in the
90 to 100 IQ range.

$$\bar{x}_1 = 84.25$$

$$Sx_1 = 18.55$$

$$\bar{y}_1 = 90.50$$

$$Sy_1 = 12.87$$

$$r_{x_1 y_1} = 0.45$$

$$\bar{x}_2 = 86.00$$

$$Sx_2 = 19.11$$

$$\bar{y}_2 = 92.13$$

$$Sy_2 = 14.37$$

$$r_{x_2 y_2} = 0.50$$

the measures. The mean scores in English at the start
of each project were 84.25 in 1973, 78.63 in 1972 and
73.77 in 1971. This indicates that the 1973 pupils
obtained 5.62 points more than the 1972 and 10.48
points more than the 1971 pupils on average. The
factors influencing the superior mean scores of the
1972 group over the 1971 group have been explained
already. In mathematics, the mean score difference was
10.37 in favour of the 1973 group. This shows the
advantage that the 1973 pupils enjoyed over the 1971
and 1972 pupils with respect to the two tests, there
again the 1973 group were different from the 1972 and
1971 pupils in attainment. One common factor of the
pupils in the six years of study was that they were of
the low SES category. Since the differences in attain-
ments between the pupils in each of the six years have
proved to be relative, this appears to define also the
relativity of the SES differences of these pupils.
Therefore in educational studies, cognitive test
classification of the subjects may yield a sharper
definition than the SES classification.

3.4   TEST OF THE TREATMENT EFFECT IN 1973

Hypothesis

The hypothesis to be tested here is that the treatment
effect is not significant. The two methods used in
carrying out the tests are the analysis of covariances
and the Sadler's t-test.

Given the tabulated F-test of f_7^7 for $\alpha = 0.05$ and
0.01 to be 0.281 and 0.196 and the computed F-test to
be 0.8253 and since $0.8253 > 0.281 > 0.196$ then the two
samples are not significantly different from each other
at beyond 0.1% level. This suggests that the gains
were not significant.

Given the tabulated F-test of f_7^7 for $\alpha = 0.05$ and
0.01 to be 0.281 and 0.196 and the computed F-test to
be 2.076 and since $2.076 > 0.281 > 0.196$, then the two
samples are not significantly different from each

other. This suggests also that the gains were not
significant. The mathematics gains were slightly
higher than the English gains. The two tests suggest
that the treatment effect was not significant in 1973.

By using the ordinary student's test for the
uncorrelated samples of the 1971, 1972 and 1973 it
turns out that the two experimental groups made
significant gains.

Analysis of covariance (1 - way) 1973 experiment

Notation

Txx = SS of x's between treatment classes	Txy = SS of y's between treatment classes	Txy = sum of product between classes
Exx = SS of x's within treatment classes	Eyy = SS of y's within treatment classes	Exy = sum of product within classes
Sxx = total SS of x's	Syy = total SS of y's treatment classes	Sxy = total sum of products

Computation table

Between Txx = 312.25	Tyy = 10.565	Txy = 11.375
Within Exx = 4963.5	Eyy = 2604.875	Exy = 22.40
Total Sxx = 5275.75	Syy = 2615.44	Total = 2251.375

Model = $Y_{ij} = \mu + \alpha_i + B(X_{ij} - \bar{X}) + \varepsilon_{ij}$

Analysis of covariance table

Source	SS	df	ms	e(ms)	f_{24}^{7} dist @ 1%
Corrected between SS	11.375	7	1.625	1.623	0.213
Corrected within SS	2240	24	93.33	93.33	
Corrected total	2251.375	31			

$$H_o : \{\alpha_1^2 = 0$$

$$H_1 : \{\alpha_1^2 = > 0 \text{ (one tailed test)}$$

Testing for the existence of a treatment effect

$$f_{14}^{7} = \frac{1.625}{93.33} = 0.213$$

1% critical value of $f_{24}^{7} = 3.50$ (one tailed test)

$$0.213 < 3.50$$

This suggests a non significant result.

Therefore there is insufficient evidence for rejecting the hypothesis that the treatment effects are the same. The result confirms the previous evidence based on Sadler's t-test for matched pairs.

As reported already, the 1972 gains were significant whereas the 1973 were not. The mean of the initial test scores were higher in 1973 than in 1972 in the two subjects. For example, the 1972 group improved from

78.63 to 83.38 or from 78.13 to 83.75 and the 1973
group improved from 84.25 to 86.00 or from 90.50 to
92.13. For further details see Table 3.4 below. These
represent different levels of improvement. But the
differences of the means scores between the 1972 and
the 1973 group reflect some elements of cultural and
cognitive difference. These two groups were similar
with respect to sex, age, SES of parents and different
with respect to ethnicity and catchment area. Also,
the 1972 group showed specific weaknesses in sentence
completion and comprehension thus indicating conceptual
and perceptual deficiencies. The 1973 group preferred
English and mathematics lessons evenly although the
boys preferred more mathematics than the girls.

Some of the problems of testing was associated with
teachers' attitude to assessment. Some teachers, for
example, objected to the testing of pupils. Changes in
the daily activities and administrative duties created
some difficulties in scheduling some of the test
sessions. Also, it was not possible to measure the
effect of motivation on the test response which would
have helped to indicate whether those who took the
tests were motivated more than those who did not take
them. The attitude of the teachers appeared to have a
strong bearing on the actual number of pupils who took
the tests.

The computation of the correlation coefficient in the
1973 study yielded $r_{x_1 y_1}$ = 0.45 and $r_{x_2 y_2}$ = 0.50. This
means that 20.25% and 25.00% of the variablity in
English can be accounted for by linear relationship
with mathematics in the before and after tests respectively. For further details see Table 3.5 below. In
1972 these were 50.41% and 43.56% respectively. This
comparison suggests that in 1972 the treatment effect
has tended to decrease the linearity between the two
subjects and in 1973 the opposite has tended to be the
case, despite the fact that the linearity between the
two subjects was higher in 1972 than in 1973. This may
indicate also that in 1972 although the scores in
English tended to predict moderately the mathematics
scores, yet in 1973 this was less so.

Table 3.4

The $\bar{x}_1$, $\bar{y}_1$, $\bar{x}_2$ and $\bar{y}_2$ computation

Scores		Before test		After test		Sample size
Region	Years	$\bar{x}_1$	$\bar{y}_1$	$\bar{x}_2$	$\bar{y}_2$	
Brixton	1970	Not tested	Not tested	Not tested	Not tested	$28C_{28}$
Islington	1971	73.77	Not tested	Not tested	Not tested	$30C_{162}$
Hackney	1972	78.63	78.13	83.38	83.75	$24C_{45}$
Addlestone	1973	84.25	90.50	86.00	92.13	$8C_{70}$
Addlestone	1974	74	75	91	82	$14C_{64}$
Camberley	1976	Not tested	Not tested	Not tested	95.36	$11C_{14}$

The above Table shows the mean scores of the 1971, 1972, 1973, 1974 and 1976 groups.

Table 3.5

The computation of the S's and r's

Test	Before test			After test		
Years	Sx_1	Sy_1	$r_{x_1y_1}$	Sx_2	Sy_2	$r_{x_2y_2}$
1970	Not tested	Not tested	Not tested	Not tested	Not tested	Not tested
1971	3.59	Not tested	Not tested	Not tested	Not tested	Not tested
1972	15.05	13.78	0.71	13.30	14.92	0.66
1973	18.55	12.87	0.45	19.11	14.37	0.50
1974	22.00	17.00	$r_{x_1y_2} = 0.68$	17.00	20.00	$r_{x_1y_2} = 0.98$
1976	Nil	Nil	Nil	Nil	Nil	Nil

The regression analysis of the English and mathematics scores in 1973 gave $bx_1y_1 = 0.31$ and $bx_2y_2 = 0.37$ for the before and after tests, thus indicating that the increase in the two subjects is a monotonic one. This indicates that the changes in the two subjects were evenly affected by the treatment effect. In 1972 $bx_1y_1 = 0.65$ and $bx_2y_2 = 0.74$. The comparison of the regression coefficient between 1972 and 1973 shows that in 1972 a unit change in one subject resulted in either 0.65 or 0.74 change for the before and after comparison, while in 1973 this led to either 0.31 or 0.37 change. This confirms the earlier interpretation that with the 1972 group improvement in one subject reflected moderate improvement in the other, whereas with the 1973 group this was not necessarily the case. Since the average values were higher in 1973 than in 1972, the above pattern may highlight the effect of the interaction between the two subjects which may be due to differences in basic skills, and in attitudes. Therefore the high initial test score in the 1973 study may reflect an effect of motivation while the low initial test scores in the 1972 one may be due to limited learning skills in English and mathematics. This reveals that while the West Indian pupils needed training in basic learning skills the English pupils in the 1973 study needed training in motivation. The analysis of the SRA individual scores shows that the 1973 pupils were on average superior to the 1972 pupils on the level of basic skill acquisition. This is supported by the previous evidence showing that the immigrant pupils were lower in reading and writing skills than the indigenous pupils.

The main elements of the basic skills are verbal, perceptual, conceptual and functioning and the rate of cognitive functioning. The motivational elements are the levels of involvement with concentration on, attention to and autonomy in cognitive tasks.

The above interpretation is supported by the following studies. Thomas (1962), Templin (1957, 1953), Irwin (1948), Anastasi (1952), Hilliard (1957) and Bernstein (1961) reported on the association between concept development and the acquisition of cognitive skills. Pringle and Tanner (1958), Davis (1937), Jenson (1963), Bernstein (1961) and Beckey (1942) reported on the association between verbal articulation and cognitive functioning. Deutsch (1964) reported on the connection between perceptual discrimination and cognitive performance. Riessman (1962) and Furneaux reported on the rate of cognitive functioning and achievement. On motivation, Deutsch (1960) reported that low involvement, concentration and attention were associated with performance while Ausubel (1963) reported that low dependence on internal discipline and high dependence on external controls were associated with learning.

The 1974 mean scores given in Table 3.4 follows rather closely the 1972 scores. The comparative figures for the 1973 study indicates that the initial test scores were consistently higher in 1973 than in 1974. The test of significance carried out resulted in a gain thus suggesting a strong effect of the programme during that year. Since the net gains were found to be significant too, this rather supports the notion of some link between the level of cognitive deficits and the potentials for an effective intervention. The correlation coefficients between the before and after test scores in English and mathematics reported in Table 3.5 show a higher level of reliability of prediction in mathematics test scores than in English. In the 1976 test scores, the mean score was higher in mathematics than the previous years and the girls tended to perform better than the boys. The boys were on average younger and less interested than the girls. Perhaps age and motivational effects rather than sex might have accounted for some of the difference in the mathematics score. The 1973 study has established that the subjects who took both the before and after tests made modest gains in English, mathematics and social skills. A close examination of the pattern of the gain has revealed that subjects with low initial test scores tended to achieve more. An attempt was made therefore in 1974 to test the hypothesis that pupils with initial low scores would tend

57

to achieve significant gains. Although the initial
test scores were lower in 1974 than in 1973 in the two
subjects yet the net gains were found to be significant
too. This has confirmed the point already made above.
Two of the poems written by a twelve and an eleven year
old have been reproduced here to indicate some aspects
of the pupils' achievement.

The Old Lady

She sits there thinking of her days in the past
She closes her eyes and remembers
She can hear the chime of wedding bells and remembers
The day that her past husband said, 'Anne will you
marry me?'
She walked down the aisle to take his hand in marriage
'I had a very happy wedding, I remember very well
But now my husband has gone up to a place where I
cannot tell

Snow

It is snowing hard
All around me
Snow flakes softly everywhere
Falling softly and silently to the ground

The ground lay white
Rooftops are glistening in the sun
I have made a snowman tall and fat
But he is melting in the sun

It is sad to see him go
He looked so nice
Oh! but what fun it would be
If it should snow all year round

But there you are
Wishes are wishes
And it doesn't snow all year round
What a pity!

Never mind though
Because if it did
We'd always be cold
And that wouldn't be very nice would it?

In the 1974 study parents were surveyed by use of
questionnaires to determine their reactions to the
programme. The analysis showed that 90% of the
respondents reported that the project had helped their
children and others thought the educational value was
high. Some of the parents said that their children had
enjoyed working with other children and that they would
help with the running of future programmes. Some
parents commented;

> 'A good scheme, jolly well done.'
> 'Debbie enjoyed the afternoons better than the
> mornings but will certainly miss the company
> when the project finishes.'
> 'The project should be available throughout the
> school holidays especially to families with
> health and social problems. It should be free
> so that those families who needed it most should
> not have an added problem of finding money to
> pay for it.'
> 'It should be available for mentally and
> physically handicapped children.'
> 'We are very pleased with this project and my
> son has thoroughly enjoyed it.'
> 'A good scheme, many thanks.'
> 'Linda has certainly enjoyed the contact with
> other children.'

The single parent families were particularly
delighted with the scheme.

3.5   THE 1972 SOCIAL ADJUSTMENT STUDY

The object of the study was to assess pupil's adjustment to schooling. In order to achieve this, the six
teachers in the project were asked to select randomly
one pupil each for intensive study. Five boys and one

girl who were black pupils were used for this study.

Observation of a girl aged seven showed that the girl tended to be distractive, showing off, attention seeking, hostile and unforthcoming. A low score was obtained on the neurological trait. The teacher described the girl to be small, poor in reading and in mathematics, mumbling and complaining of tummy aches at times. The girl was reported to be moody at times, unable to stick long on any activity. The teacher reported also that the pupil was unable to use her own initiative and she was found to be aggressive and apparently rather disturbed. The teacher went on to suggest that she might need a great deal of individual attention and supervision and that her background might have had something to do with her attitude to other pupils. The measured IQ of the girl, who was a West Indian pupil, was 74.

The account of a boy showed that he was moderately inconsequential, hostile and tended to be aggressive. The teacher reported that the boy had a great need for mental stimulation. The pupil was reported to be very intelligent by the teacher who suggested that his 'bad' behaviour might be due to an overactive mind. The teacher reported that the pupil had potential for stable responses. His measured IQ score was 113 which seemed to support the teacher's report. The pupil studied was a Nigerian aged seven.

The third pupil studied was reported to be inconsequential, hostile, erratic and aggressive with spells of violence. He tended to adopt a protective attitude towards the younger pupils and was found to stand up for his friends when they were in trouble but he tended to seek approval from adults. A visit to the boy's home revealed that his mother did not live at home with his father, and the boy was reported to spend most of his time at home on his own. His measured IQ was 75.5. The pupil was a Nigerian aged eleven years.

The fourth study of a West Indian boy aged ten years revealed that he was distractive, impulsive, hyperactive, showing off and attention seeking. The teacher who made the study remarked that the boy was unco-operative but imaginative and that he lacked confidence when in a group. The teacher felt that his own approach proved important in modifying the boy's attitude. The measured IQ of the boy was 56.5. This low IQ suggested some element of subnormality, if an IQ of under 70 was taken as subnormal.

The fifth study was made on a West Indian pupil who was reported to be inconsequential, hostile and peer-maladaptive. The study showed some evidence of a neurological trait. The teacher reported that the pupil was socially deprived and that his father did not live with his mother at home. The pupil was reported to be affective, likeable and unruly. The teacher thought that the boy needed a great deal of individual attention and affection and some discipline.

The sixth study was made also on a West Indian pupil aged eight who was reported to be inconsequential, hostile and peer-group maladaptive. The teacher reported that the boy was pleasant and could behave well if handled with care. The teacher interpreted his tensions to indicate poor maternal care and attention. This study was made by the youngest teacher of the team.

The major characteristics of the six pupils studied based on the standardised norm of the instrument used were:

1. Hostile
2. Inconsequential
3. Aggresive
4. Distractive
5. Showing off
6. Attention seeking
7. Neurological
8. Peer-maladaptive
9. Likeable behaviour pattern

This evidence was based on the analysis of the scores

on the diagnostic form and suggests that the pupils
were not adequately adjusted. The girl studied
appeared less adjusted than the boys and the teacher
reported that she was very disturbed. The two
Nigerian pupils tended to be more intelligent than the
other four West Indian pupils. The low concentration,
initiative, imagination, poor reading and poor
mathematics of these pupils may be linked with their
inadequate adjustment to school and to peers. The
teachers who did the study recommended that these
pupils needed:

1. Attention
2. Supervision
3. Mental stimulation
4. Affection
5. Discipline
6. Maternal care

These factors indicate measures of what happens at
home and in school, thus suggesting the need for an
improved link between home and school in order that
effective support can be extended to these pupils. The
educational problems of these pupils cannot be disasso-
ciated from their pattern of socialisation, with
respect to the role that parents and teachers play, in
the process towards their separate development.

The interpretation of the above study must be treated
cautiously since the instrument used had been reported
to be culturally biased. Also, the three weeks of the
observation study were not long enough to allow for
valid conclusions. The authors of the instrument have
recommended that the period of study should not be less
than one month. The strength of the data may be
enhanced by the fact that some of the teachers had had
considerable contacts with the pupils both before and
during the project.

The 1972 groups were affected largely by their low
levels of basic learning skills and poor school adjustment. The low levels of basic learning skills here
refer to the levels of the cognitive functioning which

fall below the average for their age.

3.6 THE 1972 SOCIOMETRIC STUDY

The object of the study was to establish patterns of friendship ties and the effect of the intervention programme in altering the friendship links. The pupils were given questionnaire forms both before and after the project to indicate their close friends and place of initial contact for the friendship formation. A systematic contrast was made between close friend, associate and acquaintance. For further details of this see Appendix 1. It was thought that a strong alteration of the friendship pattern in a direction towards increased preferences for the pupils in the project would indicate the positive effect of the programme. Friendship has been used here to mean the capacity to reach out to other people and the skill to retain mutual confidence. The absence of such skills through experience or pattern of socialisation could generate a sense of inadequacy or a feeling of insecurity which would inhibit responses to or offers of friendship.

Table 3.6
The ethnic structure of the pupils studied

Race	Number	Percentage
West Indians	31	63.27
English	8	16.35
Africans	4	8.16
Indians	3	6.11
Jews	3	6.11
Total	49	100.00

The 63.27% West Indian pupils were the largest ethnic group in the friendship study. The English pupils were the second largest. The proportion of the West Indian pupils in the friendship study reflected their over-representation in the project as a whole. This in turn reflected the selection pattern of the schools of the deprived pupils.

Table 3.7
The analysis of the initial place of contact

Place	Frequency	Percentage
Project	63	54.8
School	37	32.2
Neighbourhood	10	8.7
Club	2	1.7
Home	2	1.7
Church	1	0.9
Total	115	100.0

Table 3.7 shows that the pupils rated the project and school high as places of initial contact for friendship formation. Neighbourhood was placed next to these two. An analysis of the study of the homes of these pupils shows that the pupils lived in high blocks of high density council flats. These pupils tended to look more to school than to their homes and neighbourhood for the fulfilment of their social needs. Here clubs, homes and church played a minimal role as places for friendship formation.

Perhaps the high proportion of working parents, concomitant with their often prolonged absence from home during working hours, overcrowding and inadequate play facilities limited the childrens' opportunity to play together. Schools had become important to these pupils for their play. This indicates that the parts of the inner city from which these pupils were drawn are not congenial for a positive social relationship, hence these pupils have tended to use the schools as places for their emotional support much more than their homes. In such cases some of these pupils might experience role conflict if their schools failed to be sensitive to their desire for social relations. The social demands made by these pupils were experienced in the 1970 and the 1971 projects in the sense that the impact of these projects tended to be more affective and less functional. One teacher reported in 1970 that once the floodgate for emotional support was opened by the adults the pupils began to make unlimited demands. A similar experience was recorded in subsequent years.

The sociometric study was conducted separately in each of the six study groups and the results were analysed with the use of sociogram techniques. The sociograms below represent the final position of the before and after study of friendship links. Pupils were asked to choose close friends who were either in their group or outside, both at the start and at the end of the project. The results indicated that preferences for the pupils in the project tended to increase at the end of the project.

SOCIOGRAMS OF PUPILS BASED ON FRIENDSHIP CRITERION

Sociogram A revealed three isolates and one reject, two of these were West Indian pupils and one was English. The two stars were PG and MS. The friendship links expressed in this group tended to change in favour of the group members. The sociogram has depicted that the group failed to jell and this would have limited the potential for group learning and sharing of experience. This interpretation was substantiated by the teacher's account that although some learning occured in the group, there were incidents of difficult behaviour at times.

Sociogram A

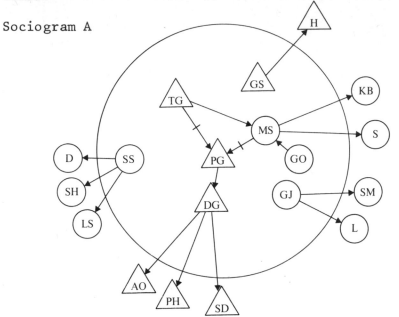

Sociogram B

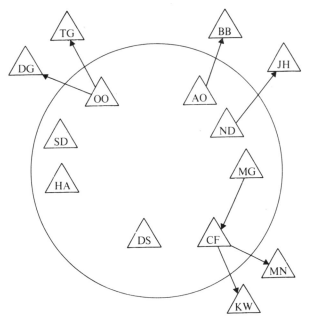

Group B was far from being a corporate unit.
Friendship tie was very low and there were six isolates
and one reject. It would not have been possible to
achieve efficient learning with the members of this
group because of the low diffusion effect. The group
was made up of boys only and was taken by a male
teacher with a favourable attitude to the project
objective. The teacher reported unsettling behaviour,
low learning activity and fights. The low friendship
preferences both within the group and between groups
indicated some elements of inadequacy or insecurity
amongst some of the group members. Preferences for
friendship links did not appear to change over the
period of the study.

Sociogram C

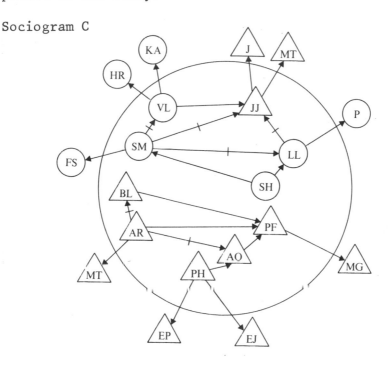

In group C preferences were observed to increase in
favour of group members. In the before test preferences were in favour of non group members but in the
after test, this was replaced by increased preferences
within the group. There were four stars in this group.
The teacher, who had a favourable attitude reported the

improvement of learning within the group and the group was high in affective achievement. There was a tendency for sub-grouping within this group which reflects perhaps that group C with ten members was rather large for an effective corporate action.

Sociogram D

There were two rejects in Group D. One was an Indian and the other a West Indian pupil reported to have displayed difficult and unsettling behaviour. The group contained one star. The friendship links tended to increase at the end of the study although the group was distinguished by its strong preferences for non group members, especially at the start of the study. The teacher was in favour of the project objective although not very keen on testing the pupils.

Group E had three stars and one isolate. Learning was reported to be high in this group, similar to group C. The teacher who had more training than the rest of the teachers although favouring the project objective was against the testing of the pupils. This group was high in both cognitive and affective gains.

Sociogram E

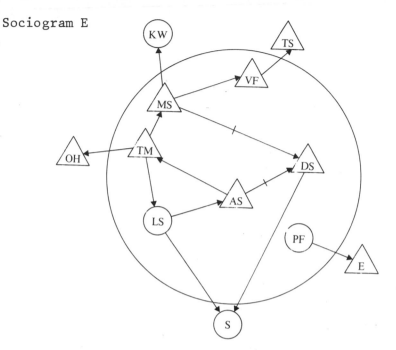

Sociogram F

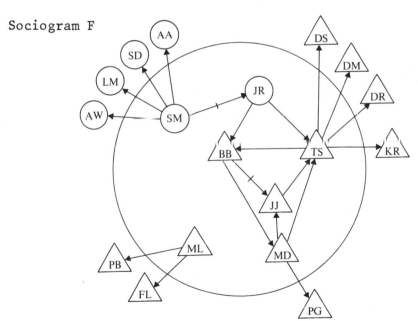

Group F had two stars and one isolate. The stars were one English and one Indian pupil. The isolate here was a West Indian pupil. The teacher reported that some learning occurred. The teacher was an Asian lady and the oldest of the team. The other five teachers were all English and only the one in charge of group B was a male teacher.

Table 3.8
The dimensions of the group structure

Group	Number in each group	Stars	Isolates	Rejects	Others
A	8	2	3	1	2
B	8	0	6	1	1
C	10	4	0	0	6
D	8	1	0	2	5
E	7	3	1	0	3
F	7	2	1	0	4

Groups B and D were low in social skills or relations. Groups A and F were moderate, and groups C and E were high.

The number of stars thrown up by each group and the level of affective gains tended to move in the same direction. The groups with high affective gains tended to achieve high cognitive gains. This was true with groups C and E and means that the group with high affective pay off in interpersonal relationships tended also to mediate a high level of learning. Some of the West Indian pupils experienced difficulties in entering into friendly social relations with other pupils and most of these were isolated from their different groups. Conflicting and unsettling behaviour patterns were experienced with these pupils. The evidence here was not at variance with the evidence revealed by the social adjustment study reported earlier in this paper. The relational study above helped in the understanding of learning processes. The sub grouping trend in group C suggests perhaps the notion of optimum group size for efficient interaction. Here a group of seven pupils would appear to yield efficient interaction.

The evidence of poor social relations amongst the West Indian pupils shown by the sociometric study in addition to the low basic learning skills and low adjustment factors already covered, might be associated with their low cognitive development. In the 1974 study the main places for friendship formation were schools, clubs and neighbourhood with schools playing a dominant part. This evidence, which is similar to the 1972 study suggests that some pupils from working class homes tended to hold a high affective expectation of their schools and experienced conflict when serious academic demands were made on them by their schools instead. The analysis of the expenditure pattern is given in the next section.

3.7 ANALYSIS OF EXPENDITURE PATTERN OF THE PROJECTS

The nil percentage of teacher's pay in 1970 and 1976 shows that the teachers were not paid in those years. The project was funded by Community Service Volunteers in 1970 and by parents in 1976. The funding of the 1971 and 1972 projects was by the Urban Programme, Inner London Education Authority and the Community Relations Commission. In 1973 and 1974 the projects were funded by Surrey Education Authority, Chertsey Urban District Council now known as Runnymede District Council, parents and private donations.

The variations in the perhead expenditure and in the percentage of teacher's pay to total expenditure result from the position that in the 1972 project teachers were paid the recommended union rates approved by the

71

ILEA and in other years the rates were locally
negotiated and related to the size of the grants. Also
the teachers in the 1972 project tended to have had
more years of training on average than in the other
years. Teachers' quality together with the level of
initial scores tended to affect the level of gains.
For example only in the 1972 and 1974 projects was the
level of gain significant. Coleman 1966 included
teachers' quality in the variables affecting attainment. The major items of expenditure were: meals,
remuneration, transportation, materials and equipment.

Table 3.9
The percentage of teachers' pay to total
expenditure and the expenditure per head of pupils

Year (i)	Total expenditure in £ (ii)	Expenditure per pupil in £ (iii)	Percentage of teachers' pay to total expenditure % (iv)
1970	100.00	3.57	Nil
1971	1,131.55	6.98	49.16
1972	983.45	21.84	68.96
1973	432.00	6.17	24.31
1974	581.00	9.08	23.23
1976	18.59	1.33	Nil

In 1970 meals and equipment were the major items of
expenditure. Travelling was limited to the local area.
In 1971, teachers' pay, materials, equipment and
transportation made up the bulk of the expenditure. In
1972 teachers' pay, administration and transportation
were the major cost items; the administration cost was

72

paid for at source during the 1971 project whereas this was not the case in other years. In 1971 and 1972 food was subsidised at source also and not in 1970 and 1973. Meals, transportation, teachers' pay, equipment and materials constituted the major items of cost in 1973 and 1974. In 1976 materials and equipment were the main cost elements. If teachers' quality and the level of initial scores resulted in significant gains as it occurred in 1972 then it would appear that by increasing expenditure on teachers' quality in terms of post experience training, significant gains in learning by some deprived pupils might be achieved. If this prediction could be validated then this would have some relevance to the development of policy strategies in education and to resource allocation in the Educational Priority Areas.

Table 3.10
The major items of expenditure

Year	Items
1970	Meals, materials, equipment
1971	Teachers' pay, materials, equipment, transportation
1972	Teachers' pay, materials, administration, transportation
1973	Meals, teachers' pay, materials, equipment, transportation
1974	Pay, outings, meals, materials, equipment
1976	Materials and equipment

3.8 CONTEXTUAL ANALYSIS

Table 3.11 shows that pupils made six hours effective

73

contact time with the teachers. This was found to be rather intensive when compared to a standard school time tabling. The pupil's social investment was reported also to be high. This was the 'floodgate' factor already covered in the analysis.

Table 3.11
The daily contact time with the pupils

Activities	Time in hours
Learning (group work)	2.30
Discovering (work-shops)	2.00
Social relations (breaks)	1.30
Total	6.00

Table 3.12
The daily training and preparation time by the teachers

Sessions	Training and preparation time in hours
Morning	00.30
Afternoon	01.30
Total	02.00

The teachers spent two hours preparing and training for the day's programme and six hours making contact with the pupils. The preparation time at home made by

74

the teachers was excluded from the computation. The
teachers reported that the eight hours daily programme
tended to make more demands on them than a standard day
in school and hence they tended to feel more tired at
the end of each day. The daily training was reported
to aid the teachers in setting daily targets. Some
teachers felt at the start of the project that it would
be easier for them to manage a group of about seven
pupils than a class of thirty. But the follow up study
of teachers' experience revealed that the demands of
the small groups were greater and that the teachers
were more exposed to their small groups than to a
classroom. The teachers thought that commitment,
evaluation, control and motivation by the headteacher
would be essential for the success of compensatory
school based projects.

Table 3.13
The weekly distribution of activity units in 1972

Week's activities	1	2	3	MT	%
Testing	14	0	17	31	12.65
Mathematics	19	15	14	48	19.59
Reading	10	7	11	28	11.43
Writing	7	2	10	19	7.76
SRA	8	7	6	21	8.57
Outing	15	11	17	43	17.55
Art	17	11	15	43	17.55
Film shows	6	4	2	12	4.90
MT	96	57	92	245	100
%	39.18	23.26	37.56	100	-

It will be seen from Table 3.13 that 12.65% of the time was taken up by testing. Mathematics occupied 19.59% of the total time. Reading and writing taken separately fell below the mathematics time. But by combining this as 'English lessons', added up to 19.19% which compares favourably with the mathematics. The activity units devoted to the SRA programme tended to be relatively consistent from one week to another but were tending to fall off towards the end of the project. This trend might have reflected the effect of its initial impact. The administration of the before and after tests inflated the distribution of activity units in weeks one and three. Some of the teachers as reported already, disapproved of devoting activity units to testing. The teachers thought that the therapeutic relationship with the pupils and the facilitating of pupils' learning were the main elements of their role. Most teachers reported that effective learning had taken place and that the discovery method used did attempt to make learning 'lighter' than it would have been in school.

The observation study of the learning processes indicates that the amplitude of the potential evoked by the discovery method approach or by the treatment stimulus tended to vary with the level of attention given to the stimulus by the experimental units. The attention level also tended to be influenced by the level of interest. Interest appeared to act as an incentive to learning. The learning intensity tended to frustrate the manifest interest. For example in 1970 a boy and a girl from different activity groups whose initial learning interest had been aroused burst into tears suddenly. A subsequent analysis of this revealed that the learning speed exceeded the pupil's capacity to control. It was found also that these two pupils tended to exchange social relations with adults more than with their peers. It would appear that besides the problem of learning rate, the dependence needs expressed by these pupils were not being met or at least recognised by the teachers initially. This incident alerted the teachers to become more sensitive to legitimate areas of the pupil's affective needs. The incident provided further material for subsequent training. The teachers agreed on a strategy to encourage dependent pupils to learn to transfer their allegiance from the teachers to their peers as a process of self-development.

3.9 THE EVALUATION OF THE TRAINING ACTIVITY

The teachers were asked in one of the training sessions to examine the implications of using teachers and non teachers in compensatory projects. Some of the replies indicated that interest and motivation to participate might not vary greatly between teachers and non teachers. What it was felt could vary was that teachers would tend to have a high educational priority and would be more likely to be in a position to relate the skills acquired to school practice. The non teachers would tend perhaps to be much less rigid, much more adventurous and much more committed to the affective aspect of the project.

On the question of whether it would be possible to raise IQ level within the scope of the project, some of the teachers thought this could occur provided the pupils were previously underfunctioning and below the level of their ability ceiling. The teachers suggested that the key factors influencing IQ growth would include the intensity of the treatment and the attack on specific learning deficits, such as word recognition, comparison and concept formation. The learning of thinking skills implicit in mathematics were reported to be a factor in raising cognitive level.

The question of the teachers' role and the factors that could influence teachers' effectiveness were examined. It was agreed that it would be essential for the teachers to play a consultative role in this process. Training activities and corporate support were seen as important factors that would help to develop teachers' effectiveness. It was also discussed in the training whether teachers would need to draw specific strengths and weaknesses out of each pupil in

77

a non threatening setting. It was accepted that the teachers had some responsibility in helping pupils to acquire skills implicit in the project objectives and that the training sessions should help the teachers in this direction.

On the forms of assessment the attitudes of some teachers to the testing were examined in one of the training sessions. Some of the teachers did not see testing as an essential part of a diagnostic approach to educational innovation. Educational innovation is used here to mean simply practices which can yield improved learning on the part of the pupils. As some of the teachers began to search for quantitative data for the assessment of their pupils, the need to use formal assessment instruments became more obvious. Some of the teachers began to see testing as part of the process influencing their strategies. One impression felt by some of the teachers that the pupils would be bored by the tests was not borne out. The critical question of the reliability of the testing instruments was noted.

Some concepts such as 'failure' and 'success' were examined for their effects on the pupils. This was done in response to the practice by which some teachers had tended to refer to pupils behaviour as 'very disturbed' during the early part of the project. The teachers were challenged to explain further the implicit meaning of 'disturbed behaviour'. One teacher said that she found it difficult to help a pupil in her group to concentrate. At this stage the discussion was centred on the need to avoid the use of stereotyped concepts. The team suggested that pupils with a concentration problem might have to be given sympathetic support. Some of these pupils were offered the option of withdrawal from the project or a change of group if they did not enjoy the activities in their own group. These pupils rejected such options and stated instead that they would prefer to try harder than they had done before. One teacher reported that the approach used in the project tended to motivate efficient responses from the pupils. Some of the

conflicting behaviour reported by the teachers included
shouting at others, jumping about, kicking and fighting
others, refusing suggestion and staying moody. The
older boys were found to be more disruptive than the
younger ones. It was suggested that some of the unsettling behaviour might be overcome if pupils were
involved in planning the daily programme. It was also
thought that the encouragement of the less bright
pupils by the bright ones and the sharing of pupils
problems within the groups might improve learning.

4 Discussion

4.1 THE LIMITATION OF THE RESEARCH

Some of the limitations of this research discussed
already include the inadequacy of the theory of
deprivation, the problem of control design in human
sciences and the difficulty of isolating the Hawthorne
effects. In addition to the above, other factors such
as sampling, research objective and testing posed
different problems. It was argued that the existing
knowledge on the nature of educational deprivation was
inadequate for the establishment of a theory of
deprivation. This made it technically difficult to
develop predictive measures that could be useful in
identifying and remedying learning deficits. It was
neither technically feasible nor ethically permissible
to design the research experiment with a built in
control of treatment and of effect within the strict
scientific conditions. Butcher (1968) and Bowlby
(1967) had drawn attention to this level of problem.
Therefore in designing the present study some attempt
was made to build into it a pilot and a control study
at different phases of the study.

In 1970 for example the pilot design was implemented
and in 1971 the control design was attempted. The
design of the first two years of the study yielded some
indexes of deprivation for subsequent operation. For
example, it was found that pupils receiving free school
meals and those who had not taken any paid family
holiday with their parents away from home tended to
experience learning difficulty and behaviour problems
in schools. The majority of the pupils who were
selected by the schools tended to fall into this
category. The pupils selected were found to experience
conflicting attitudes towards some teachers and towards
some pupils in the project.

The above design could not have been scientific

enough in minimising errors. For example, the random
method of selection was not used in selecting either
the pupils or the schools and although some care was
taken to write to all the schools in each region the
selection of the pupils tended to yield samples of
children that could be considered as extreme and perhaps biased. Some of the schools written to did not
select any pupils for the project. It might be
possible to suggest that the schools with a zero
response rate could have had some pupils who would
have qualified for the project but factors such as the
attitude of the head teachers perhaps resulted in the
schools' failure to select these pupils. All the
schools that participated in selecting the pupils
tended to rely on personal judgement. In practice the
pupils with unsettling behaviour and poor school performance were often selected for the project.

The major objectives of the research study were
related to measures of cognitive gains. The Headstart
experience indicated that experiments which were
directed to treating specific deficits, such as
language difficulty tended to prove more effective.
The wider objectives of treating other aspects of
ability domains were more difficult to assess. In
addition, some of the intervention programmes were
reported to generate the halo and the Hawthorne
effects. This resulted from the fact that the experimental units tended to react as active rather than
passive agents in the process. It was neither
practical nor even possible to measure empirically and
to isolate the above variables. Annett (1969) indic
ated this problem by stating that the novelty effect
of programmed learning could mask other effects. Since
the pupils were not told before hand that they would be
tested and since they did not expect that evaluation
tests would be given, it was possible to think that the
cue effects of the test – retest would have been
reduced.

The technology of testing also provided its own
limitation. Some of the measuring instruments used in
this research were reported to be culturally biased

and some of these measuring instruments contain social class bias. In addition some of the cognitive testing instruments were not sharp enough to discriminate between achievement scores and ability. Mosteller (1967), Kain and Hanuschck (1968) reported on this same problem. The experimental intervals of this research did not compare favourably with some of the Headstart programmes which went on much longer and yet resulted in non-significant gains.

The factors discussed above imposed severe limitations on the results of the research. It could be argued perhaps in this case that if the errors generated by the method adopted in designing this research were less than those related to methods based purely on subjective tools, then this approach would more than justify the adoption. But whatever improvement had been attempted in designing the study, any inferences drawn from this research would have to be treated with caution and seen as an exploration rather than as a definitive statement. Therefore the significant gains achieved in the 1972 and 1974 projects would have to be treated with caution. For example, some of the gains reported might have reflected improved test scores or fusion effect rather than the result of cognitive growth. Also, the results were not predictive of school success. Zimilies (1970) reported that the gains might reflect effort to improve test scores rather than effort to generate cognitive gains. These limitations suggested the existing gap between methodology and child development theory.

The Headstart experience indicated that even where the gains were reported to be significant, the effects did not seem to last. For example, McCandles and Spideer (1967), Weikart, Kamii and Radin (1964) and Clough (1972) reported that the gains were not retained. Clough (1972) and Jencks (1973) reported that in the majority of the cases the Headstart programme did not yield significant gains. The experience of the present study indicates that gains tended to reach a peak at the middle phase of the project. The research result indicates also that the groups with high initial

scores tended to make less gains than the groups with
low initial test scores. One possible explanation
might be that for those with the significant gains,
environment might have acted as the threshold factor
and as the ability ceiling was reached the rate of
gain began to decline, further treatment therefore
tending to yield less and less gains. In 1972 and
1974 the pupils who made significant gains obtained
lower initial test scores than the 1973 pupils.
Although the 1972, 1973 and 1974 pupils were similar
with respect to the SES of parents, by treating each
variable such as family size, overcrowding, parental
education, attitudes and occupations, neighbourhood
and school, separately it appeared that the 1972 and
1974 pupils were lower on each of these scales than
the 1973 ones. This suggested that pupils with severe
environmental deficits would tend to benefit more from
a compensatory programme than those relatively less
severe. Gahagan (1970) reported on the positive
relationship between actual gain and the treatment of
a specific deficit area. Furthermore, besides the
effect of ability on attainment tests as explained
already, this study has shown that specific cognitive
deficits are associated with certain levels of cognitive performance. A low level of cognitive functioning
appears to be linked with deficits in basic learning
skills such as verbalisation, perception, conceptualisation and cognitive speed. A moderate level of
cognitive functioning appears to be linked with
deficits in motivation such as involvement, concentration and autonomy. While the West Indian pupils
tended to display a greater deficiency in basic
learning skills the English pupils displayed a stronger
motivational deficiency. This suggests that while the
West Indian pupils experienced difficulty with basic
learning skills the English pupils experienced
problems of motivation. Further research is needed to
test the hypothesis that a low level of basic learning
skills tends to affect the immigrant's school attainment while motivation appears to be a factor affecting
attainment with the indigenous pupils.

4.2 THE RESEARCH AND THE HEADSTART PROGRAMMES

The present research is similar to some of the Headstart programmes with respect to the criterion measures, the measuring instruments, the programme duration, the teacher - pupil ratio and the method of treatment. The major differences include selection, scheduling of programmes, maturation level of the target population, operational and research design and the programme assumptions. Of these the major contrasting variables are the maturation level and training. Some of the differences have been discussed already in the review. But for the present short comments will be made on the maturation level, the programme scheduling, the method, the assumption and the training.

The summer months were chosen for the present study, unlike some of the year round Headstart programmes, partly for technical reasons and partly because of the experience of the earlier research studies. It was found to be technically difficult to implement the research during term time and the choice of the summer holidays reflected the consideration of evidence that during the summer holidays home and neighbourhood tended to affect the literacy of some pupils. The Turner and the 1971 NFER reports indicated the adverse effect of the school holiday on the literacy of the deprived pupils.

The age of intervention was three years on average in most of the Headstart programmes and nine years on average in the present research. The present study had discarded the genetic assumption of limited mental ability. Training formed a major part of the present study. Another major contrasting feature is the fact that while the evaluation of the Headstart programme was retrospective that of the present study was planned. The Headstart study was severly criticised on methodological differences by Young and Whitty (1973). Gain and Watts (1970) stated that the retrospective evaluation study resulted in a weak control. One major aspect of the evidence of the present research is shown

below in the Table 4.1. This Table shows that while
the treatment effectively succeeded in narrowing the
gap between the two experimental groups, it tended to
achieve the opposite effect with the within group
comparison. For example, while the between groups
differences of the 1972 and 1973 groups narrowed from
5.62 to 2.62 in English and from 12.37 to 8.38 in
mathematics, the 1972 within group differences
increased moderately by 1.75 in English and 1.63 in
mathematics. The comparison of the 1973 and 1974
figures gave a similar pattern of trend. This
indicates the paradox of increasing the within group
differences in an attempt to reduce the between group
differences. Cain and Watts (1970) also pointed this
out in their attack on the Coleman report, that the
treatment effect could result in raising the mean level
at the expense of widening the distribution. This
phenomenon appears to constitute a major philosophical
problem in education where the main principle is to
reduce educational inequality.

Table 4.1
The mean differences

Subject	English		Mathematics	
Year	Before	After	Before	After
1973	84.25	86.00	90.50	92.13
1972	70.00	83.30	78.13	83.75
Differences	5.62	2.62	12.37	8.38
1973	84.25	86.00	90.50	92.13
1974	74.00	91.00	75.00	82.00
Differences	10.25	5.00	15.00	10.13

Evidence from studies in the USA has indicated a
difference of 15 points between whites and blacks on
measures of IQ in favour of the whites. Chapter 1 of
the text contains an account of the criticisms of the
reported measured difference. Jencks has reported
also that about 67% of all American children usually
have IQ scores between 85 and 115. In England about
93% of the West Indian pupils studied had IQ scores of
between 70 and 80 which is much lower than the range
of the American children. Further evidence (see
Chapter 2) recorded has suggested that the American
blacks as a group are more deprived than the English
blacks. However, the West Indian pupils as a group
have compared less favourably with some of the
American blacks studied on measures of test scores.

As reported elsewhere in the text, the present study
was based on pupils aged on average nine years. In
the USA Headstart programme the recorded age of the
target population was on average three years. The
experience of the British programme suggests perhaps
that the maturation age of nine years is more likely
to offer greater potential for test reliability. This
factor, together with the emphasis that was placed on
the training of the adult workers and on the planned
monitoring as discussed already, constitutes the main
strength of the study. Chapter 4 contains further
evidence of the way that this study benefited greatly
from the USA experience.

The knowledge of the major characteristics of the
successful compensatory education programme in the USA
have been utilised and this has influenced the methodological design adopted for the present study as
reported in Appendices 14 and 15 of the present text.
In applying the model referred to already, the quest
has been to invoke a practical and measurable intervention programme sufficiently relevant both to the
goals of the study and to the needs of the disadvantaged pupils who participated. The two successful
programmes reported in the USA are the Peabody College

Programme and the Bereiten-Engelmann Academic
Preschool Programme. The Early Training Project was
conceived of primarily to provide field experience to
graduate students in a school psychology programme at
Peabody College in Nashville, Tennessee. However, the
dearth of information about child development and the
growing awareness of the need for such knowledge
provided an incentive to expand the programme. The
Bereiten-Engelmann Academic Preschool Programme
originated at the Institute for Research on Exceptional Children at the University of Illinois. The
monitoring of the two programmes were found to be much
more systematic and hence the associated effectiveness.

Posners study in the USA has indicated that careful
planning, clear statement of objectives, small groups,
a high degree of individualisation of instructions and
materials that were relevant and closely linked to
programme objectives, high intensity of treatment and
teacher training in the methods of the programme were
the improtant characteristics differentiating successful effort and formed their policy recommendations
accordingly. Some of Posner's more important
recommendations are that:

1. Objectives should be clearly defined and
   systematic procedures and time schedules
   for the implementation of plans should be
   set up.

2. Instructions should be individualised by
   various means such as one to one relationship
   between teacher and pupils.

3. Funds should be allocated at all maturation
   levels of preschool, elementary and secondary
   activities.

In designing future programmes, it is essential to
recognise that an objective self-evaluation by those
who plan and carry out the programme may constitute the
most important part of the processing and monitoring
functions. This picture is simulated in the figure

below.

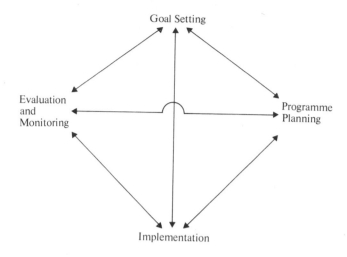

Figure 4.1 Model design of evaluation and monitoring system for programme improvement

The model above makes it flexible enough for programme organisers to be able to respond directly to feedback from the children, the parents and other participants on the programme and to modify the programme and its techniques. A systematic recording is a necessary condition for monitoring the participants responses and for statistical and content analysis.

4.3 GAIN

The 1972 and 1974 treatment effects were significant while the 1973 one was not. This has posed a number of questions. The early interventionists have tended to propose the existence of some association between significant gains and the age of interventions. One of these suggests that significant gains are consistent with preschool intervention.

Chazan (1963) reported for example that the effect of treatment was higher with boys aged 9 to 11 years than with those aged 13 to 14 years. One is led therefore to expect low probability of significant gains with early adolescents than with the kindergarten children. But the Headstart evidence did not appear to substantiate the early interventionist position. Besides, some doubts have been expressed on both the validity and the stability of preschool test scores. It seems therefore that the specific problem posed by the different levels of effectiveness obtained in the 1972 and 1973 studies may reflect more the methodological and diagnostic weaknesses rather than purely the effect of the age of intervention. While it may be argued that the older the pupils the stronger the cumulative effect of early deprivation, in order to settle the dispute systematically one will need to replicate the intervention programmes with specific age bands.

It has been stated already that the initial score of the 1973 group was higher than that of the 1972 and 1974 groups. This variability between the three groups suggests on the one hand different levels of initial basic learning skills and on the other different levels of cognitive functioning. This in turn reflects different levels of deprivation. Havighurs (1966) and Jensen (1967) had commented on the phenomenon of relative deprivation. Carney (1963), Belfield (1963) and Stott (1971) reported that the more the disadvantage the greater the chances of gain. This suggests therefore that on average the West Indian pupils experienced a stronger cognitive handicap than the white pupils. In the former this has tended to reflect a limitation of experience of the basic learning skills and in the latter a problem of motivation.

The 1973 white pupils were reported to be superior to the 1971 and 1972 West Indian pupils on their initial test scores by 10.48 and 5.62 IQ points respectively. In mathematics the differences between the 1972 and the 1973 experimental groups on the initial test scores was 12.37 in favour of the white pupils. This gives the mean difference of 9.49 points. Jencks reported that the difference between the blacks and the whites in the USA was 15 points in favour of the white. This limited evidence indicates that the effect of the inequality of educational opportunity between the blacks and white may be more pronounced in the USA than in the UK. Townsend (1973) reported on the ability structure in schools that the white pupils in the UK were superior to the West Indian pupils.

Some of the explanations given for cognitive differences included variations in language, birth rate, patterns of marriage, child minding and rearing, occupational status of the parents and discipline. Jackson (1973), for example, reported that the main characteristics of the West Indians included sub-normality, variations in dialect, unmarried and working motherhood and illegal child minding practices. Woods (1972) reported that the unsupervised children of working mothers exhibited impoverished cognitive development. Rutter (1973) reported also that the immigrant children did more chores at home, were more self-reliant, more restricted and that their parents tended to exercise a stronger discipline than the white ones. Wedge and Hilary said that family size was a factor in school achievement. The evidence of the present research indicates that some of the immigrant pupils had a limited experience of extra school activities. Although sociological variables have been found to be common with some whites yet the evidence of their impact has tended to be relative.

Besides the above factors psychological factors, such as the limited experience of basic cognitive skills based on the limited and culturally biased test scales, have been found to be associated with attainment. A further study is needed to show how the deficiency of the West Indian pupils' verbalisation, conceptualisation, perception and autonomy can

influence cognitive attainment. For some solution to
the handicaps of these pupils, Pringle et al. (1966)
and Stott (1971) suggested that the provision of early
schooling and the extension of extra-support to the
families might reduce the effect. The author's
experience indicates that unless these families can be
helped to understand and to learn to utilise such
levels of help, the net effect may be limited. For
example, during the follow-up studies some of the
families interviewed expressed conflicting attitudes
to their children's education and some tended to shy
away from offering legitimate or specific information
condusive to their need satisfaction. The evidence of
the friendship study indicates that schools can play
an important part here.

Musgrove (1966) reported that middle and late
adolescents favoured home and club for friendship
formation. This might be true of the more able
pupils, but in the 1972 friendship study, the early
adolescents expected to meet their emotional needs in
school. This difference in evidence appears to result
from variations in sampling and in pupils characteristics. One example here is that some of the Musgrove
subjects were drawn from grammar schools whereas all
the 1972 pupils came from ordinary state schools.
Therefore for most of the 1972 pupils with conditions
of overcrowding at home and limited home care, schools
have replaced home as centres for need satisfaction.
The failure by the schools to be sensitive to the
pupil's expectation can lead to role conflict. Some
of the teachers who participated in the project
favoured the need to develop affective relationship
with the pupils. The follow-up study in the Autumn of
1972 indicated that the schools from which the
children were selected were positively in favour of
increasing learning opportunities for the deprived
pupils. The experiences of the 1970, 1971, 1973, 1974
and 1976 were not dissimilar. Of the teachers'
experience, the less experienced ones tended to be
receptive, sensitive and enthusiastic whereas the more
experienced teachers found the experience dramatic,
challenging and useful. The re-examination of the

91

teachers' role and method was aroused by the project, as stated by the teachers.

The social adjustment study by the teachers in 1972 yielded profiles of extraversion, dependence, and attention seeking. Banks and Finlayson (1973) reported that these traits tended to correlate with low attainment. The motivational attribute was not measured by this scale. This was a weakness. The clustering of these factors indicated some link between learning and personality traits. The nature of the association was not established by the available research data but the West Indian pupils studied appeared to be less adjusted to school and to peers when compared with the norms of the social adjustment guides.

The study has shown that early intervention, if effective, might succeed in reducing the cumulative effect of a delayed action. It has portrayed also the over representation of working class children as a group in some deprived communities and the concomitant risk implicit therein. Parry (1974), recorded in the Times that the majority of the 25% increase in juvenile arrests in Britain, according to police report, had come from the more deprived areas. Disruptive tendencies have been linked to poor cognitive achievement also by the Bishop of Southwark, Mervin Stockwood. Pattie (1974) stated that many parents have tended to take a limited interest in their ten year old children and that there was some increase in the number of fatherless children who were being brought up in poverty with the consequential disadvantage in starting life. The 1973 and 1974 projects in which schools, Social Services and Youth Services jointly identified and treated pupils with the reported handicaps, could be one method of extending limited resources to children at risk in the deprived communities. It would appear from the result of this study, that the establishment of a multi-disciplinary organisational structure sufficiently flexible to allow for a systematic screening of children with learning and health difficulties for special attention, might form the basis for future development. Schools would need to obtain objective information about the pupils, and teachers could be given the facilities and skills to diagnose the needs of the pupils systematically. If this were the case, it would be more likely that some practical action would be taken to remedy any deficits. There were some children in the present study who would have benefited more from being referred to other types of specialists for treatment. Some of the Headstart programme focused attention on the health aspect of disability. The responsibility for helping under-achieving pupils to raise their threshold levels in learning, given adequate resources, would appear to rest largely on the combined efforts of both parents and teachers. In 1974 when parents were encouraged to become involved with the programme, this enhanced the opportunity of sharing with these parents the experience gained and their practical help was valued highly by the teachers.

The study has recorded some evidence of separation associated with children of married workers. Bowlby argued that physical separation was an important variable in maternal deprivation although the permanence of its effect is disputable. Other studies have suggested that separation is linked with diminished opportunities for parent – child interaction and reported this interaction as a prerequisit for emotional stability and linguistic development. Jensen reported that subjects with the IQ range of 60 to 90 points were culturally deprived The Bowlby Jensen model provides some sort of deprivation index. In the 1971 and 1972 studies about 87.5% and in the 1973, 1974 and 1976 about 47.6% of subjects would have fallen into Jensen's index. This picture suggests that of the subjects in the study, the proportion of deprived pupils in the London programmes was almost double those in the Surrey ones. This interpretation supports earlier analysis which indicated that the London subjects were relatively more deprived than the Surrey ones.

The main benefits of the study seem to have been shared by the children's parents, and other participants. Pupils' expectations at the start of the programme varied from 'I have come to a play centre', and 'Mummy asked me to come', to 'it is a kind of school'. Pupils' limited understanding of the programme did not seem to cause undue anxiety at the start since the settling in periods were sharp, informal and stimulating. The group activities stimulated self-expression, creative interaction and learning. The morning sessions tended to raise the within group interaction while the afternoon sessions enhanced the between group social exchanges. This had the advantage of increasing pupil's confidence and learning speed. Some children who completed course tasks correctly were observed to admire their achievements. The nature of the group tasks and manifest interest on the part of the pupils seemed to influence the quality and style of interaction. Most of the pupils were stimulated more by the social than by the academic skills content of the programme. Miller, Swift, Fletcher, Newsom and Plowden have argued that working class pupils have tended usually to shy away from academic work in some instances. One girl in the project said that she preferred the project to school.

Most of the parents reported that they would like to see the programme made a permanent feature during the school holidays. The supervisors and leaders reported that they enjoyed the demands, in terms of the training, preparation and contact time, made on them by the programmes which were heavier than the pressures of teaching. The team was encouraged by the improvement that the children made. Head teachers and parents talked of there being a real need for the programme. Except for the non-motivated older boys with which the supervisors had to exercise some discipline, the opportunity for choice, flexibility and self-orientated programmes helped to minimise the temptation to resort to the use of power in order to enforce application. This helped to make the programme enjoyable to the children. The field work practice helped to widen knowledge and offered an opportunity for increased social relations. The informal and friendly atmosphere gave pupils the chance to legitimise their demands on the adults. One supervisor reported that the stimulus provided by the experience had broken down temporarily a number of barriers and one felt this should be the first step up the ladder of a programme for progressive development.

The programmes studied during the six years were strategically sited in essentially working class communities, especially in the London area. The impressions gained so far seem to suggest that these families differed as a group from other social class groups with respect to their style of family life, value system and aspirations. Some of the families tended to become ambivalent about the social system and were dependent to some extent on the state. Marx, (1976) reported in his study of an immigrant town in Israel, that the programme of social welfare support managed by bureaucrats succeeded in creating dependency, tutelage, aggression and violence amongst the immigrants. It might be interesting to replicate a similar study in England, in order to establish the nature of the link between social security benefit, its administrative processes and the self autonomy of the recipients who depend largely on it.

The account given in Chapter 1 under school and home effects indicates the limited value so far of school reforms and the need for more positive action. The Newson study reported by Jerman (1977) has shown that bordom, work pressure, frustration in the classroom, shouting teachers, faulty locks on lavatories and undressing publicly for physical exercise are some of the factors stated by about 50% of the mothers interviewed as causes of their children's reluctance to go to school. Also, the seven year olds have become alienated because of lack of school support. Fogelman (1976) stated that adolescents from the working class homes studied spent 65% of their leisure time watching television. The Community Relations Commission Report (1974), found that the black school leavers who were reported to be low attainers educationally were influenced largely by the unsatisfactory system of school practice, disadvantaged background and poor teacher - pupil relationship. Jelinek's (1977) study suggests that Asian pupils have shown a positive attitude to multi-racial schooling although the older children have displayed less favourable attitudes.

Høgmo and Solstad (1977) have said that some pupils found the mandatory curriculum irrelevant. Compulsory schooling has tended to prevent some pupils from experiencing what might be important for future life in the community. The exclusion of the values of pupils from the formal curriculum has had a detrimental effect on the internalisation of the values and attitudes on which education is based. This has led to rebellion and has defined for the pupil what is, and what is not, important knowledge. Besides the often retrogressive effects of the selective function of formal education for further and higher education, the process has also created dependency and a feeling of worthlessness. Høgmo and Solstad have suggested that formal education is, therefore, not functioning in the interest of the plural society. This has given rise to the situation where in a stressful situation, people turn to welfare agencies rather than to neighbours, for help and support. The experience which portrays formal education as distant, irrelevant, and humiliating has generated a crisis of identity. One needs to understand the disaffected pupils within their sets of reference and to help to make these explicit by the learning process. Høgmo and Solstad question the nature of the impact that formal education has on pupils values, future life and occupation. In some cases the traditional teacher - pupil role and curriculum centred teaching have tended to make pupils passive. It is important therefore, according to Høgmo and Solstad, that the content, method and aims of education should have as their starting point an explicit knowledge, and that teaching should be pupil centred. The relevance of education is defined within this context in terms of the acquisition of community knowledge, the promotion of social change, and the attainment of personal development. The child centred

or subject initiated learning strategy advocated by
Høgmo and Solstad, has been reported by Lawson and
Jarman (1977) to have connection with Jensen's theory
of level 1 ability. The theory has indicated the
relationship between memory and subject initiated
learning processes.

Ekholm (1976) reported that context was an important
factor in learning. The major elements are communication pattern, power relationship, focus, reward system
and group structure. These factors are reported to be
central to the management of learning. A report by
the Inner London Education Authority (1977) indicated
that backwardness, emotional disturbance and deprived
homes were some of the problems encountered with the
pupils studies. Emotionally disturbed pupils were
observed to create teaching problems in the classroom.
The study shows that about 16% of the school age
population within the authority's area needed special
attention. Of these, 3% attended special schools and
13% received help in the ordinary schools. Ghodsian
and Calnan (1977) found that children receiving some
help in the normal schools made more progress than
those in schools for the educationally subnormal.

Keogh (1975) suggested the importance of making
subtle distinctions when attempting innovation. In
Chapter 1, family size was reported as one major
variable associated with school attainment. Davie
Butler and Goldstein (1972), Douglas (1964) and
Fogelman (1975 have reported on the negative effect of
a large family on school performance. Richardson
(1977) states that the correlates are more pronounced
in reading attainment than in writing productivity of
syntactic maturity. Bernstein (1972) posited that
speech systems were generated and regulated by forms
of social relations and that context was a major
control of syntactic usage. Nisbet and Entwistle
(1967) and Prosser (1973) made the point that children
from large families reported to be poor readers, on
average received relatively less verbal stimulus from
their parents. The Inner London Education Authority's
study indicated that working class pupils as a group

tended to underfunction orally. The evidence reported
so far presents a strong case for giving some sort of
systematic support in the form of a preventive
service, to pupils who are disadvantaged, in order to
raise their educational chances.

Wynn and Wynn (1974) reported that the Finnish
preventive service resulted in a reduction of the
proportion of handicapped children. Davie, Butler and
Goldstein (1972) found in Britain some discrepancy
between social classes in attendance at clinics with a
bias in favour of the middle class. Accessability of,
attitude to, ignorance of and low confidence in the
service are some of the factors restraining visits to
clinics by some working class mothers. This has
resulted in the exclusion of the children who are most
in need of protection, according to Wedge and Prosser
(1973). The World Health Organisation (1967) found
that parents ignorance was a strong factor in a
child's handicap. The Times Educational Supplement's
November 25, 1977 account of the National Consumer
Council Research by Robin Simpson states that the
child care needs produced by separation, single
parenting, working mothers and urban decay have not
been met. The Inner London Education Authority (1977)
reported that 'there was a good deal of dissatisfac-
tion with the length of time that children with
psychiatric/psychological problems had to wait for
assessment and treatment Schools were concerned about
the effectiveness of the support offered by the Child
Guidance Clinics and the Educational Welfare Service'.
Since the infant school project was found to prove
more effective than the junior school ones, evidence
which confirms the efficacy of early intervention, the
authority has suggested the need to establish a
systematic screening procedure for an early identification of children with learning difficulties.

The importance of monitoring an intervention
programme in Britain in which compensatory education
programme can be used for its coverage has become more
apparent as demonstrated by the present study. The
institution of 'linked records' as suggested by Smith

(1968) and the Inner London Education Authority (1977) might constitute an essential component of the intervention system. Since child development has been caricatured as a joint function between home and school, it is likely that a compensatory education programme could help the disadvantaged pupils to link home with school more positively. The operation of the intervention programme might have to be concomitant with the run down of special schools in order to integrate pupils with exceptional needs in ordinary schools. It would be necessary also as part of the system to substantially extend and strengthen programmes which were school and community based, together with subject orientated learning. The involvement of parents, voluntary organisations and communities, would have to be central to any intervention programme. The experience of the present study has shown some availability of goodwill, talents and time within the community, that could be rallied to complement the work of the schools if adequate thought and planning were made by local education authorities. The major conditions for an effective programme as indicated by the current study are the relevance of the programme to the participant needs, its functionality, teachers quality, school organisation, curriculum relevance, corporate or team spirit, friendly climate and planned monitoring. If treatment were directed to specific deficit it would be more likely to achieve some development of the subjects. Some of the primary conditions necessary for effective programmes have to relate to the need to:

1. Specify the deficit to be treated in a simple and measurable form.

2. State the objectives and assessment criteria precisely.

3. Establish statistical methods for quantifying treatment effects and predictive norms.

4. Relate learning to pupils experience, interest and needs as a starting point, monitor

abstract operation on lines similar to a
modified scheme of Piaget's developmental
stages, and utilise methods of learning by
discovery.

5. Organise the action sequences into
    preparation, processes, evaluation and
    feedback.

6. Select pupils for small nurturing groups of
    about seven, with enhanced opportunities for
    pupils initiative.

7. Maintain some balance between affective and
    cognitive orientations with some opportunity
    to share and examine pupils value and
    concepts.

8. Ensure that teacher's role is directed
    towards the facilitation of pupils'
    learning.

9. Make the discipline and reward system
    explicit and open and monitor individual
    pupils' progress.

10. Install a programme of systematic induction,
    regular training and feedback seminars for
    adult workers throughout the period of the
    programme.

11. Collaborate with relevant agencies in the
    selection of children and planning of
    programmes.

12. Site programme centres strategically in
    order to accommodate children with specified
    needs.

13. Procure in advance the materials and
    learning aids required for the programme.

14. Involve the selected children with the

daily planning and programming.

15. Encourage the bright children to help the
    less bright ones in the learning activity.

Strategies for improving educational chances of deprived children

Some attempts have been made by social scientists, in
response to concern expressed on the ineffectiveness
of the educational system in reducing inequality of
opportunity, to investigate and question some of the
implicit philosophical contradictions inherent in the
aims and practice of education. The limitation
relates to the efficacy of present knowledge rather
than being a reflection of any limitations intrinsic
in the disadvantaged children themselves. Nursery
schools and child guidance practices, the value system
and the inadequate methodology in the evaluation of
educational programme are some of the inherent weaknesses. Theoretically, some functionalists have
suggested, at least in part, that school practice is
based on certain needs imposed by society upon its
members. Durkheim has argued that society creates
social being with the values, behaviour and traditions
of the society. When pupils fail to respond to the
'mainstream' of educational values, prescriptive
labelling or symbolic gesture are resorted to not as a
basis for sharpening perspectives but rather as a
rationalisation of ineptness.

The dichotomy of control and development implicit in
the aims of education and the interpretative mode of
curriculum design have imposed some limitations on the
attempt to establish systematic criteria both for the
examination of educational aims and the evaluation of
its practice. The consequence of this according to
some dialecticians relates to the alienation process
that the control aspect of educational practice has
tended to yield. The inability to respond to the
'valued consensus' is interpreted by some conflict
theorists to imply a discrepancy in adaptation and
socialisation patterns on the part of the disaffected

group or category. On the problem of evaluating educational practice, some psychological instruments and factors or traits have been criticised for being rather limited in value. It appears, at least at the present, that more vigorous studies are needed to rediscover the individual as a unit with the right to be informed and to question. The philosophical problems of value and fact in educational aims, as discussed already, can be examined somehow by monitoring educational practice, embodying a mixture of both formal and informal operations, as demonstrated by the present study.

Equally the relevance of genetic and environmental perspectives to educational attainment, the function of assessment in education, the link of health and nutrition to development and learning, the acquisition of language, reading and numerate skills and the task of evaluating educational innovations do have some important bearing on the strategy for change. Pre-school screening and a diagnostic programme for early education have proved to be relevant to the needs of the disadvantaged children. The Headstart and the early intervention programmes in the USA did cover factors such as culture, heredity, instrumentation, paediatric care, neurological and psychological evaluation and language acquisition.

Some of the Headstart programmes placed emphasis on free play, perceptual training, language development and custodial care. The multi-dimensional design technique adopted was found to encourage the integration of affective and cognitive orientated learning experiences. The environmental components included medical care, parent participation and community involvement. The present study did not include the medical components in its design. Future programmes might need to make some attempt in applying health, neurological and nutritional knowledge to learning. The importance of giving children adequate nutrition was experienced rather indirectly as children on the project who became increasingly dependent on the meals provided during each programme were also tending to display generally improved dispositions. It seems relevant therefore to include all major components associated with child development in the design of future programmes.

Knoblock and Pasmanick have indicated the relationship between health status and school adjustment with low income negro children in Baltimore. The link between impaired health or organic disfunctioning and school attendance, learning effectiveness, developmental rate and personality growth and the vulnerability of the low income groups to malnutrition are some of the evidence necessitating a joint attack on deprivation by the family doctor, schools, hospitals, clinics and parents. The experience which exists of detecting extreme forms of abnormality readily could be extended to cover all other types of disability as a rule. As we have seen countries like Finland (Wynn and Wynn 1974) have been recorded as having formal procedures for preventing childhood handicaps and some important policy development by the UK Government is called for in this area. In educational planning the policy of identifying health defects or malfunctioning could be as critical as the design and management of learning experience relevant to the treatment of the deficits. The younger the age of intervention the more likely that the cumulative effects would be ameliorated. This implies the need to develop special compensatory education support on the lines suggested which can help to focus attention on the needs of the deprived children and to prepare them for the challenge of the class room.

More work is needed in the assessment of pupils at all levels in general and of the exceptional group in particular in order to establish norms for improved predictions and treatment. The use of the test battery in the study was an attempt to establish some predictive norms. One important aspect of the study has been the knowledge of functioning differentials between affective and cognitive processes and their effects on learning. This knowledge can help teachers when designing a future learning programme. Unlike

103

some of the evaluation methods of the Headstart
which concentrated on measures of changes related to
cognitive skills, the present research relied both on
cognitive and affective measures for its evaluation.
This has had the advantages of indicating the patterns
of the constituent and respondent behaviours. The
knowledge of the nature of the impact of the programme
on school, family and community is a necessary
although not a sufficient condition for the methodological development of future research. The method of
approach adopted in the study has provided the facil-
ity for highlighting factors favourable for intervention and categories of subjects likely to benefit.
An approach of this sort could change the focus from
education per se to processes and self-correcting
techniques involving an open dialogue between pupils,
teachers and parents at different levels of educational activity.

   The monitoring of pupils' performance in schools
after a period of involvement and the administering of
evaluation of class room processes may require changes
in both the concept of education and the role of the
teacher. It may help to minimise the isolation of
some schools and make them become more relevant to the
needs of the pupils and the community. As pressures
from the inner city schools increase and as research
makes learning needs and teaching practice more
explicit, greater demands should be made on those
involved in managing learning experiences. The notion
of relevance would make education more accountable to
the pupils and the community it should be designed to
serve. It is hoped that the present study has
provided some basis for discussions and explorations
relevant to further studies and improved programmes.

5 Summary

This research was directed towards assessing changes
in attainment during each year of the study. In order
to do this, pupils were withdrawn from the school
setting in the summer holidays and given intensive
compensatory treatment. Learning by discovery method
was used. The learning of English, mathematics and
social skills were the main subject areas tested.
Pupils need remained the central focus for the programme and for the therapeutic activities that
followed. The systematic appraisal and the regular
feedback of knowledge of the monitored results
influenced subsequent research planning. The explor-
atory exposure of the pupils with the preplanning of
the follow-up study of experience, improved subsequent
programmes. The teachers were trained to exploit
pupils resilience as a basis for developing learning
skills. The teachers knowledge of the subjects
provided some opportunity for their therapeutic
interaction with the pupils.

It has been mooted that a follow-up study of pupils'
performance once they were back in school would
validate evidence of gains. Although this might be a
relevant procedure it should be stated that the
planned assessment specified in the study was limited
to programme objectives and resources. The monitoring
of pupils' performance in schools after a period of
involvement in a compensatory education programme
could constitute an important area for future study.
This would give some opportunity for testing the
'fading out' effect. The present study has been
evaluated in terms of its objectives, action content,
methodology and implications. The study has given
some chances for the understanding of some needs of
children from disadvantaged homes, it has indicated a
'model' for action and quantified achievement
criteria. It would be unrealistic to think that,
within a period of three weeks or less, measurable and

permanent change would occur along the dimensions held
to be important. What has emerged is that given the
state of knowledge of deprivation, educational attainment and the methodological constraints, it is
feasible to rely on internal validation as a model for
testing the treatment effects. The 'construct
validity' applied to this study has been based mainly
on the recording observation, and reports of the programme team and supplemented by both the personal
background study and objective tests.

Evidence from the social adjustment, sociometric and
cognitive studies offered greater scope for the understanding of learning processes as well as learning
structures. Perhaps future research in this area
might have to be directed more toward the study of the
learning processes of an individual pupil in a classroom setting as a way of developing a greater insight
into the effects of educational activity. Keddie
(1973) made the point that emphasis would have to be
placed on patterns of thought through enrichment
treatment. It might be necessary therefore to monitor
an action research during school term to discover
Keddie's patterns of gains, rather than the assessment
of aggregate gains only.

The evidence relating to the effect of environmental
differences on measured gains has been obtained indirectly by statistical inferences. There has been
nothing in the research to suggest the effect of
genetic factors since this was not the object of the
study. One cannot therefore move from assumptions of
learning opportunity based on phenotypic expressitivity
to suggesting a theory of learning without some knowledge of the genotypic penetrance. Further studies
will be needed to achieve some unity. But it seems
apparent that in the absence of severe disability some
environmentally induced trait may be crucial in the
early years of the development of a child.

Although the research study has not conclusively
established the factors affecting education and the
methods for dealing with them, certain tendencies have

been shown. The research study has shown that low SES, large family units, overcrowding, low cognitive skills, low involvement in extra school activities, limited educational experience limited maternal and emotional satisfaction, inadequate day care service, limited parent – teacher contact may be associated with school attainment. The experience of this study has indicated that evidence of classroom conflict and the absence of family holidays may be associated with cognitive disabilities.

The research has shown also that compensatory education can raise attainment, that the lower the initial test scores the greater the potential for the gains to be significant, that West Indian pupils as a group have tended to perform less well than any other ethnic group on cognitive tests, that the initial test scores have tended to predict subsequent scores, that the West Indian pupils in the study have tended to rate the schools highly as a place for meeting their affective needs, that gains have tended to be superior more with friendship group than with task group and that cognitive classification appears to be more stable than SES categorisation. The research indicates also that the immigrant pupils have tended to be affected more by limited basic cognitive skills while the indigenous pupils have tended to suffer more from low motivation to learning.

The widening of achievement criteria, the improvement of teachers quality, the treatment of specific deficits and the extension of educational support to the deprived families may increase educational chances. Future research may be aimed at both the attainment pattern and the mediating cognitive processes in order to provide a systematic theory of deprivation. The study, according to comments by one supervisor in the 1970 programme, has been a voyage of discovery.

Appendices

1   FRIENDSHIP STUDY

Friendship study scaling

Children were asked to name their close friends against other friends.

Close friends. Someone you like and meet frequently, whom you trust and rely on, and to whom you would confidentially tell your secrets - and expect them to do the same for you.

Associate. You may not go out of your way to meet this person, but if he happens to be about you would probably join up with him.

Acquaintance. Someone whom you could acknowledge upon meeting him but would not normally choose for a companion at a social occasion.

Key

$\triangle$ = Male

$\bigcirc$ = Female

$\langle\triangle\rangle$ = Member of the group but not interviewed

$\longrightarrow$ = Close friend

$--\rightarrow$ = Other friend

$\longrightarrow\!\!\!\rceil$ = Reciprocated choices

Friendship pattern of older adolescents by Leslie Button (1965).

The rejects are the group members who choose but are

not chosen by others within the group. This is the unreciprocated friendship pattern.

The stars are the group members with the highest reciprocated choices within the group.

The isolates are the group members who do not choose and are not chosen by others in the group.

2 SANDLER'S T-TEST FOR MATCHED PAIRS ON THE 1972 MATHEMATICS TEST SCORES

Before and after mathematics test scores in 1972:
Sandler's t-test

	d	d^2
1	9	81
2	13	144
3	7	49
4	-8	64
5	2	4
6	6	36
7	-1	1
8	21	441
9	-3	9
10	14	196
11	-9	81
12	-3	9
13	1	1
14	9	81
15	11	121
16	15	225
17	0	0
18	6	36
19	6	36
20	6	36
21	2	4
22	24	576
23	3	9
24	5	25

$$\xi d = 135 \qquad 2,265 = \xi d^2$$

$$(\xi d)^2 = 18,225$$

$$A = \frac{\xi d^2}{(\xi d)^2} = \frac{2,265}{18,225} = 0.1243$$

$$0.266 > 0.163 > 0.1243$$

$\therefore$ The gains in mathematics are significant at both 5% and 1% levels of significance.

3 SANDLER'S T-TEST FOR MATCHED PAIRS ON THE 1972 ENGLISH TEST SCORES

Before and after English test scores in 1972:
Sandler's t-test

	d	d^2
1	-8	64
2	6	36
3	13	169
4	7	49
5	8	64
6	-3	9
7	1	1
8	8	64
9	10	100
10	5	25
11	17	289
12	-8	64
13	7	49
14	7	49
15	0	0
16	6	36
17	8	64
18	2	4
19	12	144
20	10	100
21	3	9
22	5	25
23	15	225
24	-17	289

$$\Sigma d = 114 \quad 1,928 = \Sigma d^2$$

$$(\Sigma d)^2 = 12,996$$

$$A = \frac{\Sigma d^2}{(\Sigma d)^2} = \frac{1,928}{12,996} = 0.143$$

$$0.266 > 0.163 > 0.143$$

∴ the before and after tests are significantly different.

∴ the gains are significant at both 5% and 1% levels of significance.

4 SANDLER'S T-TEST FOR MATCHED PAIRS ON THE 1973 ENGLISH AND MATHEMATICS TEST SCORES

English before and after test scores in 1973

	d	d^2
1	-4	16
2	1	1
3	9	81
4	8	64
5	0	0
6	0	0
7	0	0
8	0	0

$\Sigma d = 14 \quad 162 = \Sigma d^2$

$(\Sigma d)^2 = 196$

$$A = \frac{\Sigma d^2}{(\Sigma d)^2} = \frac{162}{196} = 0.8253$$

$0.8253 > 0.281 > 0.196$

$\therefore$ the gains are not significant.

Mathematics before and after test scores in 1973

	d	d^2
1	-5	25
2	4	16
3	4	16
4	13	169
5	0	0
6	-10	100
7	3	9
8	4	16

$\Sigma d = 13 \quad 351 = \Sigma d^2$

$(\Sigma d)^2 = 169$

$$A = \frac{\Sigma d^2}{(\Sigma d)^2} = \frac{351}{169} = 2.076$$

$2.076 > 0.281 > 0.196$

$\therefore$ the gains are not significant.

No	Scores
1	74
2	77
3	74
4	74
5	70
6	85
7	76
8	73
9	70
10	74
11	71
12	76
13	76
14	71
15	79
16	74
17	73
18	73
19	76
20	81
21	74
22	73
23	70
24	70
25	76
26	70
27	70
28	70
29	73
30	70

Mean = 73.77

Standard deviation = 3.59

No	Before		After	
	English	Mathematics	English	Mathematics
1	87	100	79	109
2	64	77	70	89
3	75	73	88	80
4	87	94	94	86
5	70	86	78	88
6	109	91	106	97
7	79	83	80	82
8	74	69	82	90
9	70	73	80	70
10	68	69	73	83
11	52	57	69	48
12	85	91	77	88
13	70	69	77	70
14	70	70	77	79
15	71	72	71	83
16	66	59	72	74
17	70	70	78	70
18	79	80	81	86
19	74	68	86	74
20	111	107	121	113
21	93	105	96	107
22	106	79	111	103
23	64	67	79	70
24	93	66	76	71

Mean = 78.63   78.13   83.38   83.75

Standard deviation
    = 15.05   13.78   13.30   14.92

Beta (b_{xy})
    = 0.65   0.74

Correlation coefficient (r_{xy})
    = 0.71

$$\text{Formula for } r = \frac{\sum_{1=1}^{n} (x_1 - \bar{x})(y_1 - \bar{y})}{\sum_{1=1}^{n} (x_1 - \bar{x})^2 \sum_{1=1}^{n} (y_1 - \bar{y})^2}$$

114

	Before		After	
No	English	Mathematics	English	Mathematics
1	57	67	53	62
2	75	97	76	101
3	74	95	83	99
4	84	95	92	108
5	71	95	71	95
6	112	109	112	99
7	101	88	101	91
8	100	78	100	82
Mean =	84.25	90.50	86.00	92.13
Standard deviation =	18.55	12.87	19.11	14.37
Beta (b_{xy}) =	0.31		0.37	
Correlation coefficient (r_{xy}) =	0.45		0.50	

$$b = \bar{y} - \bar{a}x$$

$$a = \frac{\xi\, x_1 y_1 - \bar{y}\, \xi\, n_1}{\xi x_1{}^2 - \bar{x}\, \xi\, x_1}$$

115

	English		Mathematics	
No	Before	After	Before	After
1	57	90	72	80
2	67	89	49	48
3	104	96	90	101
4	95	102	80	91
5	44	94	52	61
6	105	100	97	98
7	88	108	95	101
8	85	125	100	104
9	56	78	99	108
10	77	84	67	71
11	54	68	52	60
12	99	95	74	79
13	43	61	61	68
14	66	83	68	76
$\bar{x}$	74	91	75	82

$$S_{x_1} = 22 \quad S_{x_2} = 17 \quad S_{y_1} = 17 \quad S_{y_2} = 20$$

$$r_{x_1 x_2} = 0.68 \qquad r_{y_1 y_2} = 0.99$$

Table of mathematics test scores in 1976

No	Mathematics
1	110
2	109
3	95
4	70
5	70
6	79
7	95
8	97
9	101
10	110
11	113
$\bar{y}$	95.36
$\bar{y}_g$	104.6
$\bar{y}_b$	93.13

Key

$\bar{y}_g$ = girls mean score

$\bar{y}_b$ = boys mean score

9 BRISTOL SOCIAL ADJUSTMENT GUIDES

A Bristol social adjustment guides

The social adjustment instrument has been described as
being useful in assessing behaviour disturbances in
pupils aged five to sixteen years in school settings.
The instrument has been reported also to be culturally
biased. The social adjustment guide is reported to be
widely used in clinical studies, counselling and
assessment of treatment. The data generated by the
instrument if used per se may be limited. Its main
value appears to occur when such data can be used as
additional information to other objective data.

The instrument was used in the study in order to
obtain additional evidence of pupils' behaviour and to
sensitise the teachers on the dynamics of child
development.

B Child study, teachers' instruction

Select a boy or a girl in your group, randomly, who is
not clearly maladjusted.

Obtain your information by informal interviewing of
the pupil and by discussion of the project with other
members of staff.

Do not single out the pupil for special attention
and do not let him know that he is the subject for a
study. If for example you give a test, tell the pupil
that you are trying out the test and that you are
inviting his help.

10 HOLBORN READING SCALE

The Holborn Reading Scale is designed for measuring words recognition and reading comprehension. The 33 sentences are arranged in order of difficulty with definite scores at fourth errors.

The instrument was developed from C. Burt's Mental and Scholastic Test and P. Ballard's Mental Tests.

The main weakness of the Reading Scale is of a general kind reflecting the difficulty of measuring progress in reading through meaning and experience of a passage of prose and poetry.

1. A film of children's thought and language supplied by the Central Office of Information was used. It was the 'Looking at Reasearch' series which described how psychologists at Edinburgh University were investigating children's learning processes. Teachers who saw the film thought that it helped in generating discussions on methods.

2. Why mathematics. This was the Department of Education and Science film aimed at the 12 to 14 year olds of average ability, but with little interest in the subject. The experience indicated that the content was above the level that the pupils on the project could assimilate.

3. Learning motive. This film showed how children in the 7 to 11 age groups could be introduced to concepts of measurement in metric units of length, area, volume, capacity and weight. Pupils and teachers showed a positive interest.

4. Primary teaching - point of view. This film based on a community approach to education showed some simulations on the actual learning processes associated with creative and stimulating learning. The film generated ideas and the teachers discussed their impressions during training sessions. This film was of a particular interest in that it sensitised some of the trends and dimensions already highlighted by the project.

Reading test B.D. Age range 7.00 to 10.4 and 10.0 to 11.4. Time 20 minutes. Reliability = 0.94 (SEm 2.5). This is a reading comprehension test of the sentence completion type. It consists of 44 items presented in a continuous form and graded in order of difficulty.

Reading test A.D. Age range 7.6 to 11.1. Time 15 minutes. Reliability = 0.94 (SEm 3.6). This is a test of reading comprehension of the sentence completion type consisting of 35 items graded in order of

difficulty. Children are instructed to underline the
one word that will best complete the sentence given
from five alternatives.

Mathematics attainment test B. Age range 8.6 to 9.8
Reliability = 0.92 (SEm 4.4). This is an orally
administered test which has been found not to
discriminate between poor and good readers.

Mathematics attainment test A. Age range 7.0 to 8.6
and 7.0 to 8.1. This is an orally administered test.

Picture test 1. Age range 7.0 to 8.1. Reliability
0.92. The material is presented in three sub-tests.
The first section contains 15 items each consisting of
5 line drawings, one of which 'doesn't belong'. Each
item of section 11 shows a pattern or story in
pictures to be completed by children by underlining
their choice from the five alternatives offered. The
third section presented analogies in pictorial form.
The total number of items is 60.

Science Research Associates

The SRA laboratories are boxes of reading materials
graded to allow pupils to work at their own level.
The boxes are designed to take account, both of the
reading age and of the interest of the pupils. The
boxes consist of Power Builders which are short
stories followed by exercises on comprehension and
vocabulary; Rate Builders; which are short stories on
which questions have to be answered; and Listening
Skills Builders which are stories read to the class
and on which the pupil will answer questions from
memory. Phonic names are available also in the word
games laboratories.

   The materials are arranged to meet individual
pupil's performance level. The starting level for
each pupil is 70% score on the starter. The starter
will help the pupil to establish a procedure. The
basic steps include reading, answering questions and
checking. A consistent high performance will indicate

the pupil's readiness to progress to the next colour.

The checking of scores by individual pupils has the disadvantage of giving rise to cumulative errors since the self-checking exercise is not necessarily self-correcting. In order to overcome this the teacher may have to be diagnostic in his counselling of a pupil's progress. A score which is less than 75% will be low for further reading.

In starting a pupil, a colour below the frustration level will be chosen as a starter. This means beginning work at the pupil's level of reading attainment. The frustration level will occur when a pupil's score is 10% below the highest score and when the pupil will depend increasingly on the teacher.

The suppliers have argued that the Reading Laboratories could raise the level of pupils' reading skills through intensive use over a period of one term. In order for this to take place the pupils will be expected to have acquired an initial level of reading skill. The teacher will also have to know the limitations and learning levels of every pupil in order to achieve some efficiency. The reading age for the word builders and sentence completion is about seven years.

The efficient use of SRA may result in some economy in which the high performance pupils will tend to depend less on the teacher thus giving the teacher more time to offer consultancy service to the low performance ones.

FRIENDSHIP STUDY   CONFIDENTIAL

1. Name . . . .

    Address . . . .

    Age   Male/Female   Married/Single/Engaged/Steady

2. School last attended . . . .

    School standard . . . .

3. Work - (a) Interviewee's occupation . . . .

    Grade of work . . . .

4. Have you any close friends?

    (Someone you like and meet frequently, whom you
    trust and rely on, and to whom you would confid-
    entially tell your secrets - and expect them to
    do the same for you.)

    (a) Name . . . . . m/f . . . age . .

    How long have you been friends? . . . . .

    How did you first meet him/her? . . . . .

    What do you do together? . . . .

    Where does he/she live? (District/Distance) . .

    (b) Name . . . . . m/f . . . age . .

    How long have you been friends? . . . . .

    How did you first meet him/her? . . . . .

    What do you do together . . . .

    Where does he/she live? (District/Distance) . .

    (c) Name . . . . . m/f . . . age . .

    How long have you been friends? . . . . .

    How did you first meet him/her? . . . . .

    What do you do together? . . . .

    Where does he/she live? (District/Distance) . .

(d) Name . . . . . m/f . . . age . . .

How long have you been friends? . . . . .

How did you first meet him/her? . . . . . .

What do you do together? . . . .

Where does he/she live? (District/Distance) . .

(e) Name . . . . . m/f . . . age . . .

How long have you been friends? . . . . .

How did you first meet him/her? . . . . .

What do you do together . . . .

Where does he/she live? (District/Distance) . .

5. Have you any other friends?

(People you like and possible meet frequently whose company you seek, and who are more than associates* or acquaintances+ but are not close friends.)

(a) Name . . . . . m/f . . . age . . .

How long have you been friends? . . . . .

How did you first meet? . . . .

What do you do together . . . .

Where does he/she live (District/Distance) . .

(b) Name . . . . . m/f . . . age . . .

How long have you been friends? . . . . .

How did you first meet? . . . .

What do you do together? . . . .

Where does he/she live? (District/Distance) . .

(c) Name . . . . . m/f . . . age . . .

How did you first meet? . . . .

How long have you been friends? . . . . .

What do you do together? . . . .

Where does he/she live? (District/Distance) . .

(d) Name . . . . . m/f . . . age . . .

How long have you been friends? . . . . . .

How did you first meet? . . . .

What do you do together . . . .

Where does he/she live? (District/Distance) . .

(e) Name . . . . . m/f . . . age . . .

How long have you been friends? . . . . . .

How did you first meet? . . . .

What do you do together? . . . .

Where does he/she live? (District/Distance) . .

(f) Name . . . . . m/f . . . age . . .

How long have you been friends? . . . . . .

How did you first meet? . . . .

What do you do together? . . . .

Where does he/she live? (District/Distance) . .

* Associate: You may not go out of your way to meet
this person, but if he happens to be about you would
probably join up with him.

+ Acquaintance: Someone whom you could acknowledge
upon meeting him but would not normally choose for a
companion at a social occasion.

Personal Background

1. Name .   .   .   . Address .   .   .   .   .

     Age   Male/Female   Married/Single/Engaged/Steady

     Date of Birth

2. School last attended   .   .   .   .

     Present school .   .   .   .   . year   .   .
     (if still in school)

     Any posts of responsibility   .   .   .   .   .

     Other comments .   .   .   .

3. Subjects taken .   .   .   .

     Subjects you like least   .   .   .   .   .   .

     Subjects you like most   .   .   .   .   .   .

     Subjects you would like to follow .   .   .   .

4. Occupation or week-end or holiday employment   .

     Grade of work .   .   .   .

     Training commitments   .   .   .   .   .   .

     Previous jobs .   .   .   .

     Any ambitions .   .   .   .

5. Family background

     Father's occupation   .   .   .   .   .   .

     Mother's occupation   .   .   .   .

Brothers	Sisters
Age School/occupation	Age School/occupation

Movement of family during childhood:

Any other information offered about family experience
and background, e.g. stability?

6. Other further education . . . .

7. Other affiliations (clubs, societies) . . .

8. Church attendance: yes/no   Denomination .

9. Interests – present . . . .

               past . . . .

               would like to follow . . . .

10. Friends in the Project . . . .

Other information:

Report by . . . . . . date . . .

13 RECORDING

Recording by supervisors and researchers

.......day   date...... centre   .... recording by ..
                          or place

Climate of learning activity ....

1. Work undertaken
    (A critical and clear statement of how you spent
    your day is required here)

Time		Function	Persons involved	Comment
From	To			

2. Contacts and discussions with helpers/members of
    staff.
    This gives you an opportunity of seeing the way in
    which you helped and stimulated the work of other
    adults and how you encouraged them to use their
    time. You will also be able to keep a record of
    the plans and decisions you agreed with them.

Persons concerned	Matter	Comment and action taken/required

3. Contact and discussions with members

As you record you will build and construct a
picture of how much responsibility you have
delegated to pupils and the kind of support you
have offered them. You will also wish to note
your dealing with disciplinary matters and the
personal councelling you have done.

Persons concerned	Matter	Comment and action taken/required

4. Observation

Also you will wish to note behaviour and events
you have observed which did not involve you in
some direct action, seemingly trivual events may
suggest a great deal.

Persons concerned	Matter	Reflections/action required

5. Any other matters for recording

A space is included here in case you may wish to
report additional material.

NOTE

Recording objective is to develop skill enabling you
to penetrate beneath the surface of passing events and
to build up a sensitivity to what is happening to
individuals or groups of people. In particular we
should be interested in our own behaviour as workers,
the influence we are having and the opportunities we
may be missing.

It should include some analysis of the situation and
reflection about future action.

It should serve as a basis for discussion with
colleagues and with any one who can help the worker to
gain insight into ones situation and action.

14 TRAINING STRUCTURE

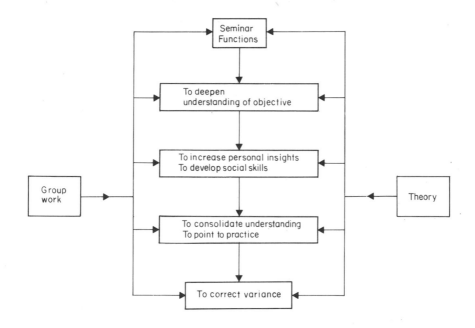

INFORMAL MEETING OF ISLINGTON SUMMER PROJECT WORKING
GROUP

Held at 212A West End Lane at 7.0pm on Tuesday 20th
April, 1971.

Present:

>   Robert, Sidney, Patrick, Margaret, Moses
>   Mr R. Baldy, Brunel University
>   Mr Sidney Samuel, Brunel University
>   Dr Patrick Quinn, Tavistock Institute
>   Miss Margaret Bray, Assistant CRO
>   Mr Moses J. Ntuk-Idem, Project Director

Apologies for absence:

>   Mr C.R. St. Hill, CRO

Points raised:

1. The need to plan the project
2. The need to establish clear objectives
3. Choice between educational and recreational emphasis with its implications
4. The evaluation methods to be used

Critical Factors:

1. The number of pupils involved
2. Selection and training of leaders
3. School involvement
4. Parents' involvement
5. Assessment criteria
6. Final report

The general opinion was in favour of an educationally orientated project.

Reasons were:

1. Pupils can benefit more from it
2. It will be different from normal holiday projects
3. It will be developmental

Organisation: The Director and the Assistant CRO should participate together in programming the project.

15 PROGRAMME

1. <u>Venue</u>. 102, Manor Road, London N 16.

2. <u>Date</u>. From July 24th to August 11th, 1972.

3. <u>Participants</u>.

Pupils	40 aged 5 to 11
Teachers	6
Organiser	1
Staff	1

4. <u>Activities</u>. Reading, writing, mathematics, art, games, plays and outings.

5. <u>Operation</u>. Pupils would be divided into six activity groups each with a teacher. The teacher would engage the pupils in learning activity through informed group work approach.

   As a vehicle for work, each pupil would be given support and friendship and nurtured to develop a repertoire of learning responses.

   Each activity would be used therapeutically in stimulating experience and in relating the experience to learning. The pupils' self-autonomy and initiative would be encouraged.

6. <u>Organisation</u>. The project would run from Monday to Friday of each week.

   The day would be divided into morning and afternoon sessions. The morning session would be held at the project centre while the afternoon would be devoted to educational study visits.

   All activities would be done in groups with teachers accompanying their activity groups.

   The lunch break would run from 12.00 to 13.30 and lunch would be provided free to pupils.

7. <u>Timetable</u>.

    09.00 - 09.30 Preparation at the centre
    09.30 - 12.00 Morning session. Group work
    12.00 - 13.30 Lunch break
    13.30 - 15.30 Afternoon session. Visiting in
                          groups
    15.30 - 17.00 Training and preparation at the
                          centre

8. <u>Objective</u>.

To raise the IQ of the pupils by 0.06

To improve the learning of mathematics, reading
and writing.

9. <u>Training</u>. Monday 17th July, 1972 planning session,
4.0pm - 6.0pm, SRA reading laboratory. Trainer -
Mr Kermode, Education Manager SRA.

Wednesday 19th July, 1972 planning session,
10.00 - 12.30, Interpersonal relationship, Trainer
- Mr Peter Spink, Human Resources, Tavistock
Institute of Human Relations.
12.30 - 1.30 - lunch.
1.30 - 3.30, Teachers attitude and teaching method
to learning. Discovery method. Trainers -
Mr R Gandy, BA, Cert.Ed. PCL and Mr Peter Derlien,
Psychologist, Surrey University.

10. <u>Method</u>.

Reading: by use of the SRA reading laboratory
Writing: by programmed work, devised by the
               teachers
Mathematics: by programmed work, devised by
               the teachers

Canlo Club - Education Department, Surrey County
Council.

1. <u>Venue</u>. Canlo Club, Chertsey Road, Addlestone,

Surrey.

2. <u>Date</u>. From July 22nd to August 12th

3. <u>Participants</u>.

Pupils: 50 aged 7 to 12 - selection will be made by the headmasters and headmistresses on the basis of learning difficulties.

Supervisors (teachers): 4 - 6 by appointment.

Group leaders (senior pupils): 5 by appointment.

4. <u>Objective</u>. To evaluate the relationship between leaning process and teaching styles.

To correct pupils learning deficits.

To assess the impact of the educational stimulation.

5. <u>Curricula</u>. English, mathematics and creative studies will be offered.

6. <u>Plan</u>. The 50 pupils will be divided into four groups of twelve. Each group will have a teacher and a leader assigned to it. The leader will engage the pupils in learning and the teacher will facilitate the learning.

Learning will be child centred and will be structured informally and the teacher will stand ready for support and encouragement. The assumption made here is that pupils with cognitive deficits can improve their learning if the teachers are perceptive enough to offer warmth and friend-ship to their pupils.

Pre-testing will be administered to diagnose pupils learning difficulties and the results will be used as a take-off point.

Post testing will be administered to evaluate the overall effect.

Teachers will supplement learning aids with their own schemes.

Educational visits will be made to widen experience and to stimulate learning.

7. <u>Structure of programme</u>.

Time	00.09 to 09.30	09.30 to 12.00	12.00 to 13.30	13.30 to 15.30	15.30 to 17.00
Monday	Preparation time by teachers and leaders	Learning session	LUNCH	Visiting session	Training seminar
Tuesday					
Wednesday					
Thursday					
Friday					

8. <u>Project staff</u>.

John Fernandes - Meads County Secondary School
Susan Parnham - Meads County Secondary School
Michael Randall - Canlo Club
Moses J. Ntuk-Idem - Canlo Club

9. <u>Supporters</u>.

Canlo Club Management Committee
Youth Officer

Balance sheet 1970

Income				Expenditure	£	s	d
Grant from Community				Advertising	2	15	0
Service Volunteers				Stationery		3	2
	£	s	d	Equipment	12	16	10
	100	0	0	Food for pupils' lunches and breaks	39	2	5
				Transport	9	5	8
				Keep for volunteer	9	0	0
				Refreshment for staff	2	15	0
				Fares for outings	6	10	0
				Postage		9	0
				Wages cleaners: 5 0 0			
				Kitchen help 5 5 0	10	5	0
				Insurance for week Liability & Indemnity	7	0	0
				Balance at bank		7	11
Total	100	0	0	Total	100	0	0

Statement of Receipts and Payments 1971

Receipts

	£
Islington Borough Council	600.00
	12.60
Community Relations Commission	211.00
Inner London Education Authority	112.25
Sundry Donations	57.50
	993.35

Less Payments

	£
Salaries	556.00
Transport & travelling expenses	272.88
Boarding expenses (1)	18.00
Lunches & entertainment expenses	76.28
Supply of milk	28.67
Insurance	10.00
Advertising	2.58
Material & equipment	120.90
Printing & stationery	12.00
Postage	14.39
General expenses	19.85
	1,131.55

Balance

Excess payments over receipts		138.20
	1,131.55	1,131.55

Statement of Receipts and Payments 1972

Confidential

Receipts

	£
Inner London Education Authority	933.45*
Community Relations Commission	50.00
	983.45

Less payments

	£
Salaries	678.45
Administration	74.04
Insurance	10.60
Cleaning	15.00
Wear and tear	30.00
Miscellaneous	17.90
Training	35.00
Fares	50.30
Photographs	25.00
Materials for assessment	20.00
Subsistence allowance for 6th formers	5.00
	961.29

Balance

Credit balance	22.16
	983.45	983.45

* This statement underestimates ILEA's expenditure at source on materials and free school meals.

Statement of Affairs of Summer Project 1973

Expenditure

	£
Leaders honorarium	105.00
Sixth formers	9.00
Insurance cover	12.00
Hire of coaches etc	84.00
Equipment	94.00
Food	110.00
Postage etc	18.00
	432.00*

Financed by

	£
Grants – Surrey County Council	200.00
Chertsey Urban District Council	100.00
Others	40.00
Contributions from parents	71.00
Transfer from Dance receipts	21.00
	432.00

* Included in total of £432.00 is £167.00 which represents estimated expenditure (invoices not yet received).

Statement of Receipts and Payments 1974

Expenditure

	£
Teachers pay	135.00
Senior pupils pay	76.00
Coach outings	81.00*
Food	83.00
Cooking and cleaning	10.00
Insurance	–
Equipment	86.00**
Reading laboratory	50.00
Reading routes	25.00
Testing instruments	35.00
	581.00

Financed by

	£
Grants – Runnymede District Council	100.00
Surrey County Council	313.00***
BAC	10.00
Other Parental contributions	92.00
Proceeds form three discos	50.00
	565.00
Deficit	16.00

NOTES

* Includes anticipated expenditure of £20 re hire of coach.

** Includes anticipated expenditure of £5 re purchase of certificates, £50 re SCC supplier, £10 re Canlo expenses.

*** Includes provision for income promised but not yet received, i.e. £96 from Social Services Department, Surrey County Council.

Statement of Income and Expenditure 1976

	£		£
Course fees	18.59	Expenses	14.99
		Cash balance	3.60
	———		———
	18.59		18.59
	═════		═════

Bibliography

Ainley, J., 'The Performance of ESN Children on Tests of Topical Operations', MSC Educational Research Dissertation, University of Surrey 1972.

Annett, J., Feedback and Human Behaviour, Penguin Education 1969.

Armor, D.J., Professor Sociology Harvard University, 'Has Busing Succeeded?', New Society January 18th 1973.

Bagley, C., 'A Comparative Study of Social Environment and Intelligence in West Indian and English Children in London', Social and Economic Studies December 1971, vol.20, no.4.

Bagley, C. and Gajen Drak Verma, 'Some Effects of Teaching Designed to Promote Understanding of Racial Issues in Adolescence', Journal of Moral Education 1972, vol.1, no.3, pp.231-38.

Banks, O., The Sociology of Education, B.T. Batsford 1968.

Banks, O. and Finlayson, D., Success and Failure in Secondary School, Methuen 1973.

Bass, B.M. and Vaughan J.A., Training in Industry: The Management of Learning, Tavistock Publications s 1967.

BBC Publications, Research in the Classroom, 1969

Barnes, A.F., Creative Ability and Young People, UCS 1962.

Barth, F., Rituals and Knowledge Among the Baktaman of New Guinea, Oslo Universitetsforlaget 1975.

Beale, G., New Society December 6th 1973, p.590.

Bell, D., 'Manpower Planning', Personnel Management November 1968.

Bembaum, G., Knowledge and Ideology in the Sociology of Education, MacMillan 1976.

Bernstein, B., 'Social Structure, Language and Learning', Educational Research 1961, no.3, pp.363-76.

Bloom, B.S., Davies, A. and Hess, Compensatory Education for Cultural Deprivation, Holt, Rinehart and Winston 1965.

Brandis, W. and Henderson, D., Social Class Language and Communication, Routledge and Kegan Paul 1970.

Brierley, J., Inspector of Schools, 'The Crucial Years of Life', New Society October 4th 1973.

Brown, A., Drama, Arco Publications 1962.

Butcher, H.J., Human Intelligence, Its Nature and Assessment, Methuen 1968.

Butler, N.R., and Bonham, D.G., Perinatal Mortality, the first report of the 1958 British Perinatal Mortality Survey p.6.

Button, Dr L., Some Experiments in Informal Group Work, 1967.

Button, Dr L., Friendship Patterns of Older Adolescents, 1965.

Button, Dr L., Discovery and Experience, OUP 1971.

Cain, G.C. and Watts, H.W., 'Coleman Report', American Sociological Review 35, 1970, pp.228-42.

Calman M. and Ghodsian M., 'A Comparative Longitudinal Analysis of Special Education Groups', British Journal of Educational Psychology June 1977, vol.47, pt.2, pp.162-74.

Campbell, D.T., and Stanley, J.C., Experimental and Quasi Experimental Designs for Research, Rand McNally 1963, 1966.

Carr, B.E., 'Grouping Children in Schools', MSC Educational Research Dissertation University of Surrey 1973.

Cattel, R.B., The Scientific Analysis of Personality, Pelican 1965.

Cattell, R.B., Personality and Motivation: Structure and Measurement, Harrap 1957.

Chauncey, H., Soviet Preschool Education, Holt, Rinehart and Winston 1969.

Clough, J.R., 'Compensatory Education Programme', A Review of Research, The Australian Journal of Education 1972, vol.16, no.3, pp262-78.

Coleman, J.S. et al. Equality of Educational Opportunity, US Department of Health, Education and Welfare 1966.

Community Relations Commission, Unemployment and Homelessness: A Report, HMSO 1974.

Corvedale, Lord., 'Extra Sensory Powers', The Times

December 1973.

Coxon, A.P.M., Project on 'Occupational Cognition', University of Edinburgh Research Memoranda November 1972, no.1.

Davie, R., Butler, N.R. and Goldstein, H., 'From Birth to Seven', The Second Report of the National Child Development Study, Longman and The National Children's Bureau 1972.

Davie, R., Deputy Director The National Children's Bureau, 'Born into the Wrong Class', The Times Educational Supplement May 4th 1973.

Davies, Bernard, Gibson and Alan, Social Education of the Adolescent 1968.

Douglas, J.W.B., The Home and the School, Macgibbon and Kee 1964.

Ekholm, M., 'The SOS-Project 23, Social Development in Schools', Institute of Education University of Güteborg, Summary of Doctorate Thesis 1976.

Ellis, A., 'Dissecting Jensen's Arguments', The Times Educational Supplement October 26th 1973.

Entwistle, N.J. and Cunningham, S., 'Neuroticism and School Attainment', A Linear Relationship, British Journal of Educational Psychology 1968, vol.38, pp.123-32.

Evans, P., 'Race Relations Report Accuses Ministry of Ignorance on Immigrants' Educational Needs', The Times September 29th 1973.

Eysenck, H.J., 'A Better Understanding of IQ and the Myths Surrounding It', The Times Educational Supplement May 18th 1973.

Eysenck, H.J., 'Nurture', letter in New Society January 24th 1974.

Eysenck, H.J., Race Intelligence and Education, Maurice Temple Smith 1971.

Fairhall, J., 'More West Indian Pupils in Subnormal Category', The Guardian November 9th 1973.

Fairhall, J., 'Teenagers Tire of School Life', The Guardian January 17th 1973.

Fogelman, K.R., Britain's Sixteen Year Olds, National Children's Bureau 1976.

Fogelman, K.R., 'Developmental Correlates of Family Size', British Journal of Social Work 1975, no.5, pp.43-57.

Fogelman, K.R. and Goldstein, H., 'Factors Associated with Changes in School Attainment Between Seven and Eleven', Journal of Educational Research 1976, no.2, pp.95-109.

Friday, J., 'Extra Sensory Powers', The Times, December 1973.

Fuchs, E., 'How Teachers Learn to Help Children Fail', Transactions September 1968, pp.45-9.

Garner, J., 'Some Aspects of Behaviour in Infant School Classroom', Research in Education May 1972, no.7, MUP.

Getzels and Jackson, Wiley, Creativity and Intelligence, 1962.

Goetschieu and Tash, Working with Unattached Youth.

Good, T.L., and Brophy, J.E., 'Teacher-Child Didactic Interactions', Journal of School Psychology, 1970.

Gordon, E.W. and Wilkerson, D.A., Compensatory Education for the Disadvantaged, College Entrance Examination Board New York 1966.

Gotschalk, D.W., Art and the Social Order.

Gray, J., 'The British Attitude is Based on Error, Prejudice and Educational Smugness', The Guardian 1974.

Guardian, The, 'Priorities in Urban Education', December 4th 1973.

Gurney-Dixon, Early Leaving, The Scottish Council for Research in Education 1953, vol.XXXV, reprinted HMSO 1966.

Halsey, A.H., Educational Priority, vol.1, HMSO 1972.

Halsey, A.H., Floyd, J. and Anderson, C.A., Education, Economy and Society, Free Press 1961.

Hamlin, R., Mukerji, R. and Yonemura, M., Schools for Young Disadvantaged Children, Teachers College Press New York 1967.

Handyside, J.D., An Experiment with Supervisory Training, National Institute of Industrial Psychology 1956, Report 12.

Hargreaves, D.H., Social Relations in a Secondary School, 1967.

Harte, B., Goals for Youth Work, YMCA Project 1969.

Healy, P., 'Greater Use of Schools to Help Parents of Difficult Children Urged', The Times November 6th 1973.

146

Hedderly, R.G., 'Attainment in Black and White', The Times Educational Supplement 1973.

Hellmutt, J., 'Disadvantaged Child', Headstart and Early Intervention, vols.1,2 and 3, Brunner and Mazel 1967, 1968 and 1970.

Herbert, G., 'The Classroom Behaviour of Socially-handicapped Boys', Department of Education and Psychological Medicine, University of Newcastle Upon Tyne.

Hess, R.D. and Shipman, U.C., Early Blocks to Children's Learning, Children 1965, no.12, pp.189-94.

Hess, R.D. and Bear, R.M., Early Education, Aldine Publishing Company Chicago 1968.

HMSO, 'Training Made Easier', Problems of Progress in Industry, no.6, HMSO Reprinted 1967.

HMSO, 'A Framework for Expansion', December 1972.

Høgmo, A. and Solstad, K.J., 'The Lofoten Project: Towards a Relevant Education', Department of Social Science, University of Tramso 1977, unpublished report.

Hudson, L., Contrary Imaginations, Methuen 1966.

Illich, I.D., Deschooling Society, Calder and Boyars 1971.

Industrial Training Board, Information Paper no.2, Ceramics, Glass and Mineral Products 1967.

Inner London Education Authority, Action Research Project, 'Children with Special Difficulties', Educational Research 1976, vol.19, no.1.

Institute of Personnel Management, Perspectives in Manpower Planning, The Edinburgh Group 1967.

Jackson, B., Director of the Child Minding Research Unit, 'The Child-Minders', New Society November 29th 1973.

Jelinck, M.M., 'Multi-racial Education', Educational Research, February 1977, vol.19, no.2,pp.129'44.

Jencks, C., Inequality, A Reassessment of the Effect of Family and Schooling in America, Allen Lane 1973.

Jensen, A.R., Educational Difference, Methuen 1973.

Jensen, A.R., 'How Much Can we Boost IQ and Scholastic Achievement', Harvard Education Review 39, 1969, pp.1-123.

Jerman, B., 'Perspectives on School at Seven Years Old', John and Elizabeth Newson's Investigation of

Children Growing up in Nottingham, The Guardian
November 1977.

Johnson, K.R., Teaching the Culturally Disadvantaged,
Science Research Associates 1970.

Kagan, J., Harvard University, 'The Importance of
Simply Growing up', New Society June 14th 1973.

Kagan, J., Roseman, B.L., Day, D., Albert, J. and
Phillips, W., 'Information Processing in the Child;
the Significance of Analytical and Reflective
Attitudes', Psychology Monograph 78, 1964, no.1.

Kaye, B. and Rogers, I., Group Work in Secondary
Schools and the Training of Teachers in its Method,
Oxford University Press 1968.

Keddie, N., Tinker Tailor, The Myth of Cultural
Deprivation, Penguin Education 1973.

Kelsall, R.K. and Kelsall, H.M., Social Disadvantage
and Educational Opportunity, Holt, Rinehart and
Winston 1971.

Keogh, B.K., Social and ethical assumptions about
special education in Wedel K. ed. Orientation in
Special Education, John Wiley & Sons
1975.

King, D., Training Within the Organisation, Tavistock
Publications 1964.

Krausen, R., "IQ Test Claims to Give Blacks a Square
Deal', The Times.

Labor, W., The Logic of Nonstandard English,
Georgetown Monograph Series on Language and
Linguistics 1969, no.22.

Lawley, D.N., 'Factor Analysis', British Journal of
Psychology June 1950, vol.III, pt.II.

Lawson, M.J. and Jarman, R.F., 'A Note on Jensen's
Theory of Level I Ability and Recent Research on
Human Memory', The British Journal of Educational
Psychology February 1977, vol.47, pt.1, pp.91-4.

Lawton, D., 'The Stock Exchange is Where Bookies
Gambol', New Society January 29th 1973.

Layard, R., King, J. and Moser, C., The Impact of
Robbins, Penguin 1969.

Leapman, M., 'Negroes Taught Use of Black English',
The Times May 26th 1971.

Legge, D., Skills, Penguin 1970.

Little, A., 'A Sociological Portrait of Education',

New Society December 23rd 1971.

Little, A., 'Does Class Size Matter', The Times
Educational Supplement June 23rd 1972.

Little, A., 'From Inequality to Diversity', The
Times Educational Supplement September 14th 1973.

Little, A., 'Striking and Disturbing Evidence', The
Times Educational Supplement 1973.

Little, A., 'Unacceptable Face of Current Practice',
The Times Educational Supplement November 9th 1973.

Little, A., Mabey, C. and Burley, R., 'How to Skim
Cream', The Times Educational Supplement June 30th
1972.

Little, A. and Stern, V., 'Immigrants: Facts Hidden
by Figures', The Times Educational Supplement
October 5th 1973.

Little, A. and Stern, V., 'Problems in Black and
White', The Times Educational Supplement February
8th 1974.

Mackworth, J.F., Vigilance and Habituation, Penguin
1969.

Macnamara, J., McGill University, 'Cognitive Basis of
Language Learning in Infants', Psychological Review
January 1972, vol.79, no.1.

Marx, E., The Social Context of Violent Behaviour,
Routledge and Kegan Paul 1976.

Mathews, J., Working with Youth Groups.

Maude, B., 'How to Manage Meetings', Management Today
November 1973.

Mcdill, E.L., Mcdill, M.S. and Sprehe, J.T.,
Strategies for Success in Compensatory Education;
an Appraisal of Evaluation Research, Johns Hopkins
Press.

McDowell, D., 'Some Organizational Issues in the
Education of Minorities', (Inquiry into the
preparation of teachers for the Socially Deprived,
University of York). London Education Review Spring
1973, vol.2, no.1.

Medley, D.E. and Mitzel, D.W., 'Measuring Classroom
Behaviour by Systematic Observation', Gage, N.,
Handbook of Research on Teaching Chicago, Rand
McNally 1963.

Miller, G.W., Educational Opportunity and the Home,
Longman.

Miller, S.M., 'Review Inequality', <u>Sociology of</u>
<u>Education</u> 1973, vol.46, no.4.
Miller, D.R., and Swanson, C.R., <u>Inner Conflict and</u>
<u>Defence</u>, Henry Holt 1960.
Ministry of Education, <u>Half Our Future</u>, HMSO 1963.
Ministry of Labour, <u>Manpower Studies</u>, series nos.1-6,
HMSO 1964, 1965, 1966, 1967 and 1968.
Morrison, A. and McIntyre, D., <u>Teachers and Teaching</u>,
Penguin Education 1969.
Musgrove, F., 'The Social Needs and Satisfaction of
Some Young People', <u>British Journal of Educational</u>
<u>Psychology</u> 1966, vol.XXXX1, pt.22.
Newson, J. and Newson, E., <u>Four Years Old in an</u>
<u>Urban Community</u>, Allen and Unwin 1968.
Newson, J. and E., <u>Patterns of Infant Care in an</u>
<u>Urban Community</u>, Penguin 1965.
Newson, J. and E., <u>Four Years Old in an Urban</u>
<u>Community</u>, Penguin 1970.
Ntuk-Idem, M.J., 'An Informal Education Project',
<u>Race Today</u> July 1972.
Ntuk-Idem, M.J., 'A Schooling in Alienation', <u>Race</u>
<u>Today</u> July 1972.
Ntuk-Idem, M.J., 'Analysis of Training Activity',
<u>Social Service Quarterly</u> July-September 1973.
Ntuk-Idem, M.J., 'A Research Study of the Structure
of Components of Morality Categories', MSC Education
Research Dissertation University of Surrey 1976.
Ntuk-Idem, M.J., 'The Effect of Activities of the
Participants; Research and Analysis', Department
of Education University College of Swansea 1970.
Nygreen, G.T., 'Interactive Path Analysis', Princetown
University, <u>The American Sociologist</u> 1971, vol.6,
pp.37-43.
Passow, H.A., <u>Reaching the Disadvantaged Learner</u>,
Teachers College Press New York 1970.
Peaker, G.F., <u>The Plowden Children Four Years Later</u>,
National Foundation for Educational Research 1971.
Peters, R.S., <u>Perspective on Plowden</u>, Routledge and
Kegan Paul.
Plowden Central Advisory Council for Education
(England), <u>Children and Their Primary Schools</u>, vol.2
HMSO 1967.
Postman, N., 'The Politics of Reading', <u>Harvard</u>

Educational Review May 1970, vol.40, no.2, pp.244-52.

Postman, N. and Weingartner, C., _Teaching as a Subversive Activity_, Penguin Education 1969.

Reimer, E., _School is Dead_, Penguin Education 1971.

Richardson, K., 'Reading Attainment and Family Size; an Anomaly', _British Journal of Educational Psychology_ February 1977, vol.47, pt.1,pp.71-5.

Rist, R.C., 'Student Social Class and Teacher Expectation; the Self-fulfilling Prophecy in Ghetto Education', _Harvard Educational Review_ 40 August 1970, pp.411-51.

Roberts, J.G., _Developing Effective Managers_, Institute of Personnel Management, revised edition 1974.

Robinson, J. and Barnes, N., _New Media and Methods in Industrial Training_, 1968.

Roff, H.E. and Watson, T.E., _Job Analysis_, IMP Broadsheet 1961.

Rogers, T.A.P., 'Providing the Human Resources', _Personnel and Training_ 1968.

Rosen, B.C., 'The Achievement Syndrome; a Psychological Dimension of Social Stratification', _American Sociological Review_ 1956, XX, pp. 155-61.

Rosen, B.C., and Andrade, R.D., 'The Psychological Origins of Achievement Motivation', _Sociometry_ 1959, XXII, pp. 183-218.

Ross, J.M., Douglas, J.W.B. and Simpson, H.R., _All Our Future_, Peter Davies London 1968.

Schools Council Research Project in Compensatory Education, University College of Swansea, Department of Education, _Occasional Publications_ I, II and III 1968, 1970 and 1971.

Schools Council, Working Paper 27, _Crossed With Adversity_, Evans 1970.

Selakovich, D., _Social Studies for the Disadvantaged_, Oklahoma State University 1970.

Serpell, R., Hester Adrian Research Centre, University of Manchester, 'How Perception Differs Among Cultures', _New Society_ June 22nd 1972.

Seymour, W.D., _Operator Training in Industry_, IMP Broadsheet 1959.

Seymour, W.D., _Industrial Skills_, Pitman 1966.

Silberman, M.L., The Experiences of Schooling, Holt
  Rinehart and Winston 1971.
Silcock, B., 'What's Your Blood IQ', The Times 1974.
Smith, A., 'Linkage of Child Health Records', World
  Health Organisation Regional Office for Europe,
  Euro 0215(7) 1968.
Smith, Dr P.B., Improving Skills in Working with
  People.
Smith, Dr P.B., Groups within Organization;
  Applications of Social Psychology to Organizational
  Behaviour, Harper and Row 1973.
Smith, F., A History of English Elementary Education
  1760 - 1902, G.L.P 1931.
Stanley, B.P., 'The Correlates of Academic Success for
  the Average Child in a Pressurising Suburban
  Community', MSC Education Research Dissertation
  University of Surrey 1973.
Swift, D.F. Basic Readings in the Sociology of
  Education, Routledge and Kegan Paul, London 1970.
Tannenbaum, A.J., 'Alienated Youth', The Journal of
  Social Issues Spring 1969, vol.XXV, no.2.
Tead, O. and Metcalf,H.C., Personnel Administration,
  New York 1920.
Times Educational Supplement, 'Five Year Olds on Their
  Own', November 25th 1977, p.5.
Tizard, B., Child Development Research Unit,
  University of London Institute of Education, 'In
  Defence of Nurture', New Society January 10th 1974.
Townsend, B., Director of the Schools Council Research
  Project in Education for Multi-racial Society,
  'Training Inadequate for Multi-racial Society',
  The Times Educational Supplement September 14th 1973.
University College of Swansea, Department of Education
  Occasional Papers I 1968, II 1969.
University of York, 'Social Deprivation and Change in
  Education', Report of the Conference Organised by
  the Enquiry into Preparation of Teachers for the
  Socially Deprived, April 1972.
Vernon, P.E., Creativity, Penguin 1970.
Vernon, P.E., Intelligence and Cultural Environment,
  Methuen 1969.
Vinter, R.D., Programme Activities; An Analysis of
  Their Effects on Participant Behaviour, (2nd rev.)

1960.

Wedge, P. and Prosser, H., <u>Born to Fail</u>, Arrow Books
1973.

West, D.J., <u>Present Conduct and Delinquency</u>.

Wilby, P., 'Should ESN Schools be Abolished', <u>The
Observer</u> July 22nd 1973.

Wilton, V.M.E., University of Bradford, Postgraduate
School of Studies in Research in Education, P.G.
Squibb, Gordon Pemberton Research, 'The War of
Jencks', letters to <u>The Guardian</u> January 22nd 1974.

Wiseman, S., 'The Manchester Survey', Children and
Their Primary Schools, Report of the Central
Advisory Council for Education, vol.2, appendix 9,
HMSO London 1967.

Woods, M.B., Bryn Mawr College, Pennsylvania, 'The
Unsupervised Child of the Working Mother',
<u>Developmental Psychology</u> 1972, vol.6, no.1, pp.14-25.

World Health Organisation, 'Working Group on the
Early Detection and Treatment of Handicapping
Defects in Young Children', Regional Office for
Europe, Copenhagen 1967, pp.12-24.

Wynn, M. and Wynn, A., 'The Protection of Maternity
and Infancy', A Study of the Services for Pregnant
Women and Young Children in Finland with Some
Comparison with Britain, Council for Children's
Welfare, Spring 1974.

Wynn, M. and Wynn, A., 'The Right of Every Child to
Health Care', A Study of Protection of the Young
Child in France, Council for Children's Welfare
Summer 1974.

Young, A., 'Models for Planning Recruitment and
Promotion of Staff', <u>British Journal of Industrial
Relations</u> November 1965.

Young, M.F.J., University of London Institute of
Education and Whitly, G., School of Education
University of Bath, 'Deprivation Debate', <u>The Times
Educational Supplement</u> September 14th 1973.